LON ECONOMIC STRATEGY FOR AUSTRALIA

Magic Pudding or Enduring Solutions?

An Interim Report for CEDA

Fred Argy

CEDA

Longman Cheshire

Longman Cheshire Pty Limited
Longman House
Kings Gardens
95 Coventry Street
Melbourne 3205 Australia

Offices in Sydney, Brisbane, Adelaide and Perth. Associated companies, branches and representatives throughout the world.

First published 1992

Designed by Lauren Statham
Set in Goudy 11/13
Produced by Longman Cheshire Pty Ltd
Printed in Australia by Short Run Books

National Library of Australia
Cataloguing-in-Publication data

Argy, Fred.
A long term economic strategy for Australia.

Bibliography.
ISBN 0 582 68486 2.

1. Australia — Economic policy — 1990– . 2. Australia — Economic conditions — 1990– . I. Committee for Economic Development of Australia. II. Title.

338.994

About CEDA

The Committee for Economic Development of Australia (CEDA) is an independent, apolitical organisation made up of business leaders, academics, and others who have an interest in and commitment to Australia's economic and social development, through undertaking objective discussion and research into issues affecting Australia's growth.

About the author

Fred Argy AM, OBE

Until June 1991, Fred Argy was the Director of the Office of the Economic Planning Advisory Council (EPAC).

He had been a Commonwealth public servant since 1964, with extensive experience in several departments, including Treasury, Employment and Industrial Relations, Trade, and Housing and Construction.

He was secretary to the Committee of Inquiry into the Australian Financial System (Campbell Inquiry) in 1979–81 and Australian Ambassador and Permanent Representative to the OECD from 1983–85. He was awarded an OBE for public services in 1981 and an AM for service to national economic planning in 1992.

Fred Argy is a graduate in economics from Sydney University, where he completed B.Ec and M.Ec degrees.

Foreword

We have pleasure in presenting this interim report of *A Long Term Economic Strategy for Australia—Magic Pudding or Enduring Solutions?*.

CEDA is to be commended for initiating such a substantial program of research. The invaluable support and advice of CEDA Trustees is a clear illustration of their commitment to the favourable economic and social development of Australia through encouraging CEDA's program of research and informed debate.

We are particularly grateful to the members of the project's Trustee Advisory Committee, for their valuable advice and comment on various aspects of this report.

Constructing a vision for an Australia that works is a task of great responsibility; one which requires a thorough, rigorous approach. It requires the vision and insight of many people, including that of the project director, Fred Argy.

A key requirement in an undertaking of this kind is financial support. CEDA is particularly grateful to the major supporters of this important initiative:

- AOTC
- BHP
- NorTel Australia Pty Ltd
- Commonwealth Bank of Australia
- Deloitte Ross Tohmatsu

In a climate where so much of our thinking is dominated by short term considerations, it is doubly important to encourage a long term perspective.

We commend this interim report to you.

Eric A Mayer
Chairman
CEDA Board of Trustees

John Thom
Chairman
Citibank Limited

Co-Chairmen, *An Australia That Works: A Vision for the Future*

Contents

Acknowledgments

In May 1991 a conference in Sydney launched a major CEDA project—*An Australia that Works: A vision for the future.*

As part of this project, I was asked in September 1991 to prepare a report on the direction we need to go as a nation, the changes needed and how change can be made to happen. The report was to be prepared over a two-year period and finished by the end of 1993. The paper published here is my interim report to CEDA on this project. It discusses the issues involved in formulating a long term economic strategy and outlines some of the elements of such a strategy.

Parts of the paper benefited greatly from technical comments received from Professor John Freebairn, Professor Victor Argy and Dr Robin Stewardson. My thanks also to Professor Barry Hughes, Dr Owen Donald, and members of two CEDA panels of economists, one headed by Robin Stewardson and one by Paul McCarthy, who provided helpful comments. No doubt many faults remain and for these I alone am responsible.

As well I would like to express my appreciation for the on-going support and advice received from Eric Mayer and John Thom, the Project Chairmen. My thanks also to Lynne Reeder and various other members of the CEDA staff for the invaluable logistic support they provided.

The charts and tables were kindly prepared by Sallie McCleery from the Economics Department of BHP.

Fred Argy
Project Director

Introduction

Calls for a national vision have come from the media and from many of our business and community leaders. This paper looks at some of the issues involved in the development of a long term economic strategy for Australia.

It is necessary first to define the scope and aims of the project.

First, it is not an attempt to predict the future. Rather it is a search for a long term strategy that will give us better economic results than in the past without sacrificing other important community goals. It is an attempt to map out a better course for the future rather than to forecast it.

Second, a national vision should not be viewed as a 'wish list'. The goals must certainly be ambitious and challenging but they must also be realistic, achievable and compatible with each other. In short, *the vision must be not only desirable but feasible.*

Third, the project does not start with a presumption that there is only one true vision—like a light on the hill—and that if one looks for it one will find it. We realise there are a number of desirable and feasible visions, each reflecting different values and priorities in the community. We also realise there are multiple means of pursuing each of the visions. The aim is to examine the implications of alternative visions and strategies, and to help CEDA and eventually the community at large choose between them.

A long term economic strategy ultimately needs to have at least the broad backing of governments if it is to have any practical relevance. This means it must be capable of securing a wide base of support in the community. That doesn't require consensus. It means the mix of national goals making up the vision must be capable of commanding more support in the community than any other feasible alternative mix of goals. For this to happen the vision must recognise the multi-dimensional character of peoples's hopes and aspirations and the complexity of values in the community; it must not be too narrowly centred on monetary goals.

The long term strategy must also be responsive to changing world markets and technological and social developments, and it needs to be regularly reviewed in the light of these developments.

Why a long term strategy?

A long term economic strategy of this sort can serve a number of useful purposes:

- it can help turn public discussion and policy planning away from short term developments towards longer term goals and strategies;
- it can help us focus on the things we as a nation have been doing wrong (and right) in the past, and the broad areas where improvements are desirable and feasible in the future;
- it can help bring out the inter-dependencies and potential conflicts between the various national goals and the dangers of looking at goals in isolation from each other—the 'magic pudding' or 'cargo cult' syndromes;
- it can help us see more clearly the options which we face and provide a consistent framework for systematically exploring the implications of alternative paths and strategies;
- if the strategy has the endorsement of a number of influential people in the community and its philosophy is broadly consistent with that of the Government, it can act as a catalyst for change, making the community rethink priorities and galvanising it to greater effort and reform (the future is not something pre-ordained: it depends on human choices and actions); it can also act as a planning guide for industry and commerce;
- and finally the vision underlying the strategy can serve as a benchmark for assessing and monitoring the nation's future progress, thereby encouraging a greater sense of responsibility and accountability across the community (not just governments).

Steps towards a long term strategy

It is useful to see a long term economic strategy as evolving in nine distinct steps or stages:

- First, we need to set ourselves a set of *long term performance benchmarks or criteria.*
- Second, we must use these benchmarks to evaluate the past performance of the economy, so that we can *understand where we performed badly* and where we performed well.
- Third, we must analyse our failures and seek to *understand why we went wrong* in the past.
- Fourth, we must *determine what goals we want to achieve in the future*—our 'desirable' vision.
- Fifth, it is necessary to assess *how the various goals relate* to each other and to what extent they are compatible with each other.
- Sixth, where conflicts exist, we must work out a method of resolving the trade-offs and *setting relative priorities*, to ensure the vision is both desirable *and feasible*.
- The seventh step is to *determine an appropriate strategic role for government.*
- The eighth step is to draw up *a specific program of policy reform* (an action plan or policy blueprint) that will best achieve the desirable/feasible vision.
- Finally, an effective *plan of implementation* must be put in place.

This report is limited in scope and intent; it focuses principally on the first four steps. It suggests a set of performance benchmarks, reviews Australia's past economic performance, examines why we under-performed in some areas, and proposes some goals for the future. While it briefly explores the interaction between the goals, presents some evidence on community attitudes and priorities, and discusses the role of government in long term strategic planning, it does not offer any specific proposals for reform. The hope is that it will stimulate public discussion and assist CEDA in producing its final report late next year.

Executive Summary

CEDA's project, *An Australia that Works*, aims to develop a long term economic vision and strategy for Australia. This interim report outlines the main aims of the project and highlights some of the complex issues involved in the development of a long term economic strategy. It is hoped that it will stimulate public debate which will assist CEDA to produce its final report late next year.

A long term national economic strategy can be viewed as evolving in distinct stages. Nine steps are identified in the interim report:

- first, a set of performance benchmarks or criteria must be selected;
- second, on the basis of these criteria, the past performance of the Australian economy needs to be reviewed;
- third, past failures must be analysed and lessons drawn;
- in the light of this experience, provisional national goals must be set for the future;
- fifth, an assessment must be made of the extent to which the goals conflict with each other;
- where conflicts exist, national priorities must be set to arrive at an internally consistent vision;
- seventh, a view must be taken of the appropriate strategic role of government in furthering this vision;
- eighth, a specific program of reform (policy blueprint) must be designed;
- finally, a plan of implementation must be devised.

Although the interim report touches on all these questions, it focuses principally on the first four.

Performance benchmarks (Chapter 1)

The paper suggests six long term performance criteria: the trend rate of growth in real incomes per head; the degree of stability of incomes around the trend; the underlying rate of unemployment; changes in the distribution of incomes and wealth; improvements in the quality

A LONG TERM ECONOMIC STRATEGY FOR AUSTRALIA

An Interim Report for CEDA

Fred Argy

CEDA Special Research Project

An Australia That Works: A Vision for the Future

Part I:
A Long Term Economic Strategy for Australia - Interim Report

Executive Summary

CEDA is currently embarked on a major two-year project to develop a national economic vision and action plan for the long term. Part I of the project, A Long Term Economic Strategy for Australia, will seek to point out the choices and alternatives we face if we want a better future for ourselves and our children and grandchildren.

Project Director Fred Argy's interim report outlines the main aims of the project and highlights some of the complex issues involved in the development of a long term economic strategy. His executive summary, reproduced herewith, outlines the scope of his interim report.

August 1992

Executive Summary

CEDA's project, *An Australia that Works*, aims to develop a long term economic vision and strategy for Australia. This interim report outlines the main aims of the project and highlights some of the complex issues involved in the development of a long term economic strategy. It is hoped that it will stimulate public debate which will assist CEDA to produce its final report late next year.

A long term national economic strategy can be viewed as evolving in distinct stages. Nine steps are identified in the interim report:

- first, a set of performance benchmarks or criteria must be selected;
- second, on the basis of these criteria, the past performance of the Australian economy needs to be reviewed;
- third, past failures must be analysed and lessons drawn;
- in the light of this experience, provisional national goals must be set for the future;
- fifth, an assessment must be made of the extent to which the goals conflict with each other;
- where conflicts exist, national priorities must be set to arrive at an internally consistent vision;
- seventh, a view must be taken of the appropriate strategic role of government in furthering this vision;
- eighth, a specific program of reform (policy blueprint) must be designed;
- finally, a plan of implementation must be devised.

Although the interim report touches on all these questions, it focuses principally on the first four.

Performance benchmarks (Chapter 1)

The paper suggests six long term performance criteria: the trend rate of growth in real incomes per head; the degree of stability of incomes around the trend; the underlying rate of unemployment; changes in the distribution of incomes and wealth; improvements in the quality of life (defined broadly to include such things as leisure, health, job satisfaction, educational and cultural opportunities, law and order, quality of air and water, individual freedom, level of economic sovereignty etc.); and finally, as a rough indicator of inter-generational equity, trends in net wealth (including both human-made and natural capital and adjusting for changes in external liabilities).

This broad view recognises that ultimately an economy exists to serve the needs of society and that people's hopes, aspirations and values are complex and multi-dimensional and are not narrowly centred on material or monetary goals.

Review of past performance (Chapter 2)

The paper then examines the performance of the Australian economy over the last twenty years or so against these six benchmarks and concludes that it has under-performed on the three economic criteria—per capita growth, stability and unemployment. This economic failure cannot be explained in terms of a desire to enhance social equity, quality of life or the environment, as even in these three latter respects the record is patchy and in parts worrying. We should aim to do considerably better over the next two decades.

Factors bearing on past performance (Chapter 3)

The paper reviews the long term factors that may explain our relatively poor economic performance.

We know that we saved too little, borrowed too much, invested inefficiently, produced and exported too little, paid ourselves too much relative to our productivity, allowed our capital to remain under-utilised for long periods, were slow to adopt new technology and new ways of work, and failed to improve our human capital to the same extent as our major competitors.

These are however symptoms rather than causes. The more fundamental underlying factors are considered under seven headings:

- institutional barriers: our performance may have been held back by our federal system, our industrial relations system, our system of education and training, and the strength of sectional interests in our political processes;

- attitudinal constraints such as 'them and I' in the work place, complacency, inertia, and a management mentality that was inward-looking and which demanded and expected too much of government;
- an incentive climate (the structure of taxes, relative prices and rewards) which was not conducive to efficiency and growth, and which sent out perverse signals to the market for much of the 1970s and 1980s;
- the failure of free markets to function efficiently in some areas; this was sometimes due to insufficient information, such as in foreign exchange and credit markets, sometimes to lack of adequate competition, such as in important sectors of industry, and sometimes to a failure to give adequate weight to the interests of future generations, such as in land management practices;
- adverse external influences, such as unfavourable world markets for our principal exports;
- failures of macroeconomic policy, such as over-reliance on fine tuning and in particular on short term monetary policy; and
- arguably, the maintenance of high rates of population growth despite economic risks in the short/medium term.

In many of these areas we have seen real progress in recent years.

Provisional goals (Chapter 4)

The paper presents a set of provisional goals for the future—an illustrative vision—based on the six performance benchmarks noted earlier. The *primary* goals are:

- an underlying (trend) growth rate in real National Disposable Income per capita of at least 2% per annum—much better than the 1980s and 1970s but not as good as the 1960s; in the next few years, because of the scope for significant reductions in unemployment and improvements in productivity, a growth rate in per capita incomes of at least 3% should be achievable;
- sufficient short term cyclical stability to ensure that real GDP per head never grows by less than 1 to 1.5% in any one year;
- a return to a sustainable unemployment rate of 5% by the late 1990s;

- no worsening in the position of very low income earners, with genuine equality of opportunity for every one;
- continued improvements in the quality of life and, in particular, no further deterioration in our living environment; and
- sufficient growth in net national wealth, including full conservation of at least crucial parts of our natural environment, to safeguard the interests of future generations.

The paper then outlines a set of *intermediate* targets for investment, saving, exports, current account deficit, inflation etc. which, it is argued, need to be achieved to realise the first three primary goals outlined above, which together make up a 'growth first' scenario. This helps to bring out the potential internal inconsistencies of our illustrative vision: the difficulties of reconciling the economic goals with each other, and possible contradictions between the economic goals and the three other vision goals—distributional equity; improved quality of life and inter-generational equity—thus underlining the magnitude of the task before us.

Choices and priorities (Chapter 5)

National goals, such as the ones we have chosen, can conflict for three reasons: available resources are limited relative to the goals; the goals are often inter-dependent; and policy instruments are limited relative to policy targets.

The paper stresses the importance of searching for policies which involve 'positive sum games' i.e. which enable us to perform better in respect of some goals without sacrificing other goals. Policies which seek to promote competition, encourage better disclosure and dissemination of information, or which facilitate work place flexibility, training and structural adjustment, often fall into this category. But the scope for these is limited. Trade-offs are unavoidable.

Those designing a long term strategy must first know what the feasible trade-offs are and then try to assess the community's preferred choices and priorities.

In Chapter 5, examples are given of the kinds of trade-offs that need to be resolved, such as between the interests of present and future generations (as in the area of environment policy); between social equity on the one hand and efficiency and per capita growth on the other (e.g. when deciding on the extent and methods of redistribution sought or the pace of structural change); between low unemployment in the short term and long term stability through low inflation (as in choosing the monetary stance); and between per capita growth and stability (e.g. when deciding on the level and method of industry assistance). It is hoped that the final report will be able to quantify some of the trade-offs involved, although we do not under-estimate the complexity of such an exercise.

National priorities are basically determined through the political process. The final report will try to gauge the community's priorities by drawing on opinion surveys, including one proposed by CEDA.

Role of government (Chapter 6)

There are two contrasting views of the role of government in the development and implementation of a long term national economic strategy—the libertarian or market-based view and the statist or interventionist view. The paper leans towards a pragmatic approach which draws on both schools for inspiration. It urges a continuous review of all government interventions to ensure they are not having perverse effects on decisions to save, invest, innovate and export; but markets often do fail (as the corporate excesses of the 1980s demonstrated, for example), and sweeping opposition to all new forms of government intervention in the economy is not a logically sustainable position.

This report does not put forward any long term policy blueprint—a task reserved for the final report.

Implementation (Chapter 7)

Once a blueprint or plan of action is drawn up, the hardest task of all is to implement it. The paper notes three types of constraint—attitudinal (resistance to change), institutional (the system of governance) and technical (limited policy tools and data in a volatile inter-dependent world).

These issues are largely ones for the final report (or are to be the subject of other CEDA projects). The present interim report touches on them briefly, noting in particular the important role of consultation and consensus-building.

The future (Chapter 8)

While the paper is very critical of Australia's past economic performance, measured in terms of actual results, it also stresses the positive signs that have emerged in the last decade, especially in work place attitudes, in a greater outward orientation by business, in the willingness of the community to question long-standing institutions and beliefs and accept broad-based structural reform, and in the improved incentive climate.

While much remains to be done, the writer believes that the seeds have been laid for an economic renaissance. But hard choices will have to be made.

A Long Term Economic Strategy for Australia - Interim Report **by Fred Argy, published by the Committee for Economic Development of Australia and Longman Cheshire Pty Limited, Melbourne, August 1992. 95pp.**

CEDA
COMMITTEE FOR ECONOMIC DEVELOPMENT OF AUSTRALIA

CEDA House
123 Lonsdale Street
Melbourne, Victoria. 3000
Tel: (03) 662 3544
Fax: (03) 663 7271

124 Phillip Street
Sydney, NSW. 2000
Tel: (02) 221 5844
Fax: (02 233 6602

of life (defined broadly to include such things as leisure, health, job satisfaction, educational and cultural opportunities, law and order, quality of air and water, individual freedom, level of economic sovereignty etc.); and finally, as a rough indicator of inter-generational equity, trends in net wealth (including both human-made and natural capital and adjusting for changes in external liabilities).

This broad view recognises that ultimately an economy exists to serve the needs of society and that people's hopes, aspirations and values are complex and multi-dimensional and are not narrowly centred on material or monetary goals.

Review of past performance (Chapter 2)

The paper then examines the performance of the Australian economy over the last twenty years or so against these six benchmarks and concludes that it has under-performed on the three economic criteria—per capita growth, stability and unemployment. This economic failure cannot be explained in terms of a desire to enhance social equity, quality of life or the environment, as even in these three latter respects the record is patchy and in parts worrying. We should aim to do considerably better over the next two decades.

Factors bearing on past performance (Chapter 3)

The paper reviews the long term factors that may explain our relatively poor economic performance.

We know that we saved too little, borrowed too much, invested inefficiently, produced and exported too little, paid ourselves too much relative to our productivity, allowed our capital to remain under-utilised for long periods, were slow to adopt new technology and new ways of work, and failed to improve our human capital to the same extent as our major competitors.

These are however symptoms rather than causes. The more fundamental underlying factors are considered under seven headings:

- institutional barriers: our performance may have been held back by our federal system, our industrial relations system, our system of education and training, and the strength of sectional interests in our political processes;

- attitudinal constraints such as 'them and I' in the work place, complacency, inertia, and a management mentality that was inward-looking and which demanded and expected too much of government;
- an incentive climate (the structure of taxes, relative prices and rewards) which was not conducive to efficiency and growth, and which sent out perverse signals to the market for much of the 1970s and 1980s;
- the failure of free markets to function efficiently in some areas; this was sometimes due to insufficient information, such as in foreign exchange and credit markets, sometimes to lack of adequate competition, such as in important sectors of industry, and sometimes to a failure to give adequate weight to the interests of future generations, such as in land management practices;
- adverse external influences, such as unfavourable world markets for our principal exports;
- failures of macroeconomic policy, such as over-reliance on fine tuning and in particular on short term monetary policy; and
- arguably, the maintenance of high rates of population growth despite economic risks in the short/medium term.

In many of these areas we have seen real progress in recent years.

Provisional goals (Chapter 4)

The paper presents a set of provisional goals for the future—an illustrative vision—based on the six performance benchmarks noted earlier. The *primary* goals are:

- an underlying (trend) growth rate in real National Disposable Income per capita of at least 2% per annum—much better than the 1980s and 1970s but not as good as the 1960s; in the next few years, because of the scope for significant reductions in unemployment and improvements in productivity, a growth rate in per capita incomes of at least 3% should be achievable;
- sufficient short term cyclical stability to ensure that real GDP per head never grows by less than 1 to 1.5% in any one year;
- a return to a sustainable unemployment rate of 5% by the late 1990s;

- no worsening in the position of very low income earners, with genuine equality of opportunity for every one;
- continued improvements in the quality of life and, in particular, no further deterioration in our living environment; and
- sufficient growth in net national wealth, including full conservation of at least crucial parts of our natural environment, to safeguard the interests of future generations.

The paper then outlines a set of *intermediate* targets for investment, saving, exports, current account deficit, inflation etc. which, it is argued, need to be achieved to realise the first three primary goals outlined above, which together make up a 'growth first' scenario. This helps to bring out the potential internal inconsistencies of our illustrative vision: the difficulties of reconciling the economic goals with each other, and possible contradictions between the economic goals and the three other vision goals—distributional equity; improved quality of life and inter-generational equity—thus underlining the magnitude of the task before us.

Choices and priorities (Chapter 5)

National goals, such as the ones we have chosen, can conflict for three reasons: available resources are limited relative to the goals; the goals are often inter-dependent; and policy instruments are limited relative to policy targets.

The paper stresses the importance of searching for policies which involve 'positive sum games' i.e. which enable us to perform better in respect of some goals without sacrificing other goals. Policies which seek to promote competition, encourage better disclosure and dissemination of information, or which facilitate work place flexibility, training and structural adjustment, often fall into this category. But the scope for these is limited. Trade-offs are unavoidable.

Those designing a long term strategy must first know what the feasible trade-offs are and then try to assess the community's preferred choices and priorities.

In Chapter 5, examples are given of the kinds of trade-offs that need to be resolved, such as between the interests of present and future generations (as in the area of environment policy); between social equity on the one hand and efficiency and per capita growth on the other (e.g. when deciding on the extent and methods of redistribution sought or the pace of structural change); between low unemployment in the short term and long term stability through low inflation (as in choosing the monetary stance); and between per capita growth and stability (e.g. when deciding on the level and method of industry assistance). It is hoped that the final report will be able to quantify some of the trade-offs involved, although we do not under-estimate the complexity of such an exercise.

National priorities are basically determined through the political process. The final report will try to gauge the community's priorities by drawing on opinion surveys, including one proposed by CEDA.

Role of government (Chapter 6)

There are two contrasting views of the role of government in the development and implementation of a long term national economic strategy—the libertarian or market-based view and the statist or interventionist view. The paper leans towards a pragmatic approach which draws on both schools for inspiration. It urges a continuous review of all government interventions to ensure they are not having perverse effects on decisions to save, invest, innovate and export; but markets often do fail (as the corporate excesses of the 1980s demonstrated, for example), and sweeping opposition to all new forms of government intervention in the economy is not a logically sustainable position.

This report does not put forward any long term policy blueprint—a task reserved for the final report.

Implementation (Chapter 7)

Once a blueprint or plan of action is drawn up, the hardest task of all is to implement it. The paper notes three types of constraint—attitudinal (resistance to change), institutional (the system of governance) and technical (limited policy tools and data in a volatile inter-dependent world).

These issues are largely ones for the final report (or are to be the subject of other CEDA projects). The present interim report touches on them briefly, noting in particular the important role of consultation and consensus-building.

The future (Chapter 8)

While the paper is very critical of Australia's past economic performance, measured in terms of actual results, it also stresses the positive signs that have emerged in the last decade, especially in work place attitudes, in a greater outward orientation by business, in the willingness of the community to question long-standing institutions and beliefs and accept broad-based structural reform, and in the improved incentive climate.

While much remains to be done, the writer believes that the seeds have been laid for an economic renaissance. But hard choices will have to be made.

CHAPTER

1

PERFORMANCE CRITERIA

Before any work can start on a long term vision and strategy we need a set of performance benchmarks.

The first thing to stress is that the performance of an economy over the long term (say over a twenty year period) should be assessed not in narrow monetary terms, such as the rate of increase in national output of goods and services and physical wealth, but rather in terms of the overall wellbeing of Australians.

Human wellbeing is impossible to measure comprehensively, but there are at least six ultimate tests or criteria which can be applied.

1 Our first performance measure is the trend rate of growth in *real incomes per head*. This gives a broad indication of underlying improvements in *material* welfare—the additional goods and services available in the market which can be purchased by the population out of their incomes. (It can be argued that we should use real consumption per head rather than real incomes per head as the performance test. However, someone who decides to save more and consume less cannot be said to be worse off, even though his or her current living standards may have decreased in a narrowly defined sense. In the view of the writer, income is the more appropriate measure of national welfare.)

Per capita income is an important performance benchmark not only because material welfare is itself a major component of human wellbeing, but also because material well-being has an important bearing on the capacity of the population to divert resources to the pursuit of other values such as improvements in the quality of life and the environment.

2 Our second performance indicator is the *level of instability of incomes*, i.e. how large the fluctuations have been around the trend growth.

This is important because people generally prefer to have incomes rising steadily rather than fluctuating around a rising trend. Moreover, short term instability has a long term cost e.g. for long term unemployment, investment risk, efficiency and even in some cases for confidence in the financial system.

The relationship between cyclical stability (sustained growth) and long term unemployment is currently receiving increased attention from economists ('long and deep recessions are now seen to produce higher average unemployment in their aftermath. This strengthens the case, if such were needed, for avoiding major recessions' (Pitchford 1992)).

3 It is possible for an economy to grow quite strongly and steadily in per capita terms (e.g. because it is innovative and efficiency conscious) and at the same time experience high and even rising unemployment. Such an economy cannot be said to be successful. Our third performance test, therefore, is the long term underlying *trend in unemployment and under-employment.*

High and sustained unemployment is a symptom of failure not only because of the economic losses involved—in terms of potential output, erosion of skills, increased resistance to structural and technological change etc.—but also because of what it can mean for equality of opportunity, social cohesion and the dignity, self-respect and self-fulfilment of the individual. With most people the availability of government income support, however generous, is not an adequate substitute for a job. That is why, in many countries, employment has been viewed as a social right like freedom of speech, and this notion is built into the proposed European Community social charter.

4 It is impossible to evaluate any nation's economic performance without considering the social dimension, and in particular what has

happened to the distribution of incomes and wealth, poverty levels, the incidence of long term unemployment, the regional dispersion of welfare, and the well-being of disadvantaged minority groups like Aborigines. Our fourth performance criterion, therefore, is *changes in the distribution of incomes and wealth*, which will be taken as a rough (and necessarily imperfect) proxy for social equity.

An economy showing strong growth in average per capita incomes is not necessarily performing well if this growth is associated with growing disparities in income and wealth and increased levels of poverty. This is true even in narrow economic terms. First, welfare economists have long recognised that, where there are losers as well as winners (i.e. the losers are not actually compensated in full), the effects on overall national well-being are at best uncertain and at worst—if the initial situation was already one of wide inequality and the change was expected to increase further this inequality—likely to be perverse (Little 1960, Abelson 1987).

Second, a distribution of incomes and wealth which is perceived to be very inequitable can endanger social peace and cohesion, including law and order, with damaging effects on confidence and investment; it can thus in the end turn even the winners into losers.

Third, a social security system which provides effective safeguards against poverty can help to preserve the quantity and quality of the nation's stock of human capital during periods of adversity.

By reducing the income risk associated with economic change, such a social security system can also assist the process of economic reform e.g. it may reduce resistance to structural change and make trade unions more disposed to accept a widening of wage disparities.

Apart from such economic implications, wide income and wealth inequalities and high concentrations of economic power are not consistent with fair equality of opportunity and access, and hence with true liberty of the individual (Rawls, p. 278). Of course the absence of gross inequalities in income and wealth is not a sufficient condition for the achievement of fair equality of opportunity; it is also necessary to ensure equal access to jobs and to public goods and services, especially education.

Most Australians would in any case reject as morally objectionable a pattern of economic growth which left a significant section of the community appreciably worse off.

That said, it should be recognised that, beyond a point, the pursuit of social equality can actually reduce individual freedom (e.g. if it requires prohibitive levels of taxation or close policing of welfare eligibility); or it may so impair economic efficiency, saving, growth and stability that in the long run the least advantaged members of the community are worse off rather than benefiting. When that point is reached, further extension of the welfare system can be inequitable and counterproductive for present generations and unfair to later generations. This issue is taken up again later in the paper.

5 Our fifth performance test is changes in the *quality of life*, broadly defined as the non-market and non-material sources of enjoyment and happiness available to the existing population. These include: leisure, health, housing standards, incidence of crime, the diversity of educational and cultural opportunities available to us, the quality of the air we breathe and water we drink and bathe in, the availability of parks and wilderness, the level of noise, and the conditions under which people work (including not only the quality and safety of the physical working environment but also the extent of employee participation, mutual trust and shared commitment).

Importantly it also includes the degree of personal freedom and scope for self-advancement people enjoy, and the extent to which there is genuine equality of opportunity in employment, education etc. The quality of life of the population also depends on how much say they have in how the society is run (i.e. it implies strong democratic institutions), the degree of political stability, and to what extent they feel domestically and internationally secure and economically independent from the rest of the world.

To many people, the quality of life is as highly valued as real spending power over goods and services (real incomes).

6 Our sixth and final performance test is the total *net wealth (human-made and natural) bequeathed to future populations*, which we will take as a proxy for *inter-generational equity*.

The relevance of this is obvious: a nation may be able to show a substantial rise in real incomes, employment and quality of life over a period of say a decade, and yet during this period the population may save very little, borrow a great deal from foreigners, invest only in things with short term returns, neglect its infrastructure, and allow its natural environment to be damaged in a way which, while having no immediate effects, has the potential to severely reduce the quality of life of future populations. Has such a nation performed well?

The extent of the obligation of the present population towards its successors is a matter of controversy. 'How the burden of capital accumulation and of raising the standard of civilization and culture is to be shared between generations seems to admit of no definite answer. It does not follow however that certain bounds which impose significant ethical constraints cannot be formulated' (Rawls 1971, p. 286).

While people appear to discount future benefits relative to present benefits (see results of a survey in *The Economist*, 23 March 1991, p. 76), governments have an obligation to protect future as well as present generations and should ideally be less influenced by time preference.

Indeed one could argue that human-made capital and natural capital are not always substitutable with each other and that to achieve inter-generational equity a national economy needs to ensure *both* (i) growth in physical wealth and (ii) maintenance or betterment of at least key parts of the natural environment. This point will be taken up again later.

In the discussion above we outlined six possible performance tests for an economy.

The tests are broad-ranging in character and go beyond the kinds of indicators (GDP, employment, inflation etc.) which economists normally focus on when assessing economic performance. The approach adopted in this paper should not require any justification however. An economy exists to serve the needs of society and these needs are complex and multi-dimensional and are not narrowly centred on monetary goals.

Some readers might well ask: what about inflation, the current account deficit, productivity, savings, investment, exports, education and training. These are all of course important, but they should be viewed as intermediate rather than primary or ultimate indicators of performance.

Take inflation for example. Many have seen it as our number one problem, but when you probe you find that their concern is mainly about what inflation does to ability to sustain high and stable economic growth and low rates of unemployment, or what it does to the distribution of incomes (and especially fixed income earners). In other words their concerns boil down to one or other of the six benchmarks outlined above.

Similarly with the others mentioned. Even education can be viewed as a means to a better quality of life and higher real incomes.

These intermediate indicators will receive close analysis in the final report and they are discussed briefly in a later section of this report.

A more serious objection to our proposed set of economic performance criteria, as a basis for developing national goals for the future, is that they are too insular—that is, they are not global enough. Shouldn't we be as concerned about the *world* distribution of incomes and welfare (or at least with income/welfare disparities in our region) as with distributional equity within Australia?

Ideally we should, of course. The United Nations report on human development (1992) points to a polarisation in global wealth over the past 30 years. Unfortunately it is doubtful if any national vision which embraces the well-being of other nationals is going to have much appeal to the people or the politicians, except to the extent that it has implications for broad national security and stability, in which case it is already encompassed in the quality of life performance benchmark.

CHAPTER

2

OUR PAST PERFORMANCE

Looking back over the last twenty years, how has the Australian economy fared in terms of our six performance criteria? (The reader is referred to some illustrative tables and charts at the end of the paper.)

1 *Growth in per capita real incomes* has been quite modest both by comparison with our earlier post-war experience, and by international standards.

Per head of population, our National Disposable Income (real GDP less real depreciation, less unrequited transfers and net income paid overseas deflated by import price deflator) increased by 3% per annum in the 1960s, 1.6% p.a. in the 1970s and only 1.3% per annum in the 1980s (Treasury 1990). Of course since 1989–90, we have seen an absolute decline in per capita real disposable incomes.

In brief, our growth experience in the last twenty years has been considerably worse than in the previous twenty years, although (to put it in perspective) somewhat better than in the decades before the Second World War (Maddock & McLean 1987).

Our per capita performance also looks disappointing when set against that of other countries. Using current purchasing power parities, our real GDP per capita has slipped relative to other OECD countries: in 1970 we were 10th out of 27; in 1990 we were 13th out of 27. There appears to have been a particularly sharp relative decline in the 1980s: in 1985 Australia's per capita GDP was 2% under the OECD average, and in 1990 it was 6% under the average (ABS 5226.0 1992). It is chastening to recall that just before Federation, Australians enjoyed the world's highest living standards.

As for our East Asian neighbours, their growth rate per capita averaged over 6% in the 1980s and is expected to exceed 5% in the 1990s (*World Bank Bulletin* No.4, August/October 1991). Some of these countries are rapidly catching up with us in living standards (at least as traditionally measured). A recent study by a Japanese think tank, Nomura Research Institute, has Australia growing at only one-half to one-quarter of the rate of the six ASEAN countries over the next decade, and it has Australia's per capita output falling behind Singapore's by the year 2000 and to equality with that of Hongkong (Nomura 1989).

Australia's relative performance may be even more disturbing than it appears at first blush. This is because the growth in per capita incomes in Australia in the 1970s and 1980s was assisted by two socio-demographic developments. First, reflecting changes in age structure, there was a relatively sharp increase in people of working age relative to the total population; and second, reflecting increases in female participation rates, there was an increase in the proportion of the working age population in the labour force. These two changes in fact accounted for 1/3 of the increase in per capita incomes in the two decades in question. Yet the two factors will work less in our favour in the decades ahead (DEET 1991, p. 45).

Nor can we expect any boost to living standards from improvements in the terms of trade. (Actually, movements in the terms of trade had surprisingly little effect on the growth in incomes per head over the last two decades (Treasury 1990)).

In the next decade (unless we can reduce unemployment—an issue taken up later) we will have to rely on productivity improvements for almost the entire growth in per capita incomes. Apart from its direct contribution to living standards, our productivity performance will drive our competitive trade performance, which in turn will be the major constraint on our capacity to grow.

Unfortunately, our productivity performance, especially in the recent past, has been quite poor.

Australia's labour productivity growth began to slow down in the

1970s, and in the 1980s it grew at less than half the rate of the 1960s (ABS 1992, Phipps 1992, EPAC CP 39). It has also been slow relative to what comparable developed countries have been able to achieve (in the 1980s our productivity growth was significantly below the OECD average), and relative to that of our Asian neighbours (whose productivity growth was twice ours) (OECD and World Bank).

It is notable that Australia's real GDP per employee, adjusted for purchasing power, has slipped from 8th among OECD countries in 1970 to 14th in 1990 (OECD/Canadian Ministry of Supply and Services 1991).

Australia's low labour productivity growth in the 1980s was in part a reflection of real wage restraint, which impacted on the capital/labour ratio (EPAC CP 39, Treasury 1992, Dowrick 1990). However, a disaggregation of the productivity data casts a little doubt on the view that the slow-down was wholly or even largely a response to real wage restraint (Phipps 1992). Moreover, the evidence is too consistent to be explained solely in those terms. Whether one looks at output per worker hour, or output per worker, or at the productivity of both labour and capital combined (i.e. total factor productivity), the impression one gets is of an economy that has been underperforming relative to its past and relative to other comparable countries in the last couple of decades.

Similar impressions are gained when we look at another key source of improvement in competitiveness and material living standards—innovation or technological progress. Apart from the fact, already noted, that growth in total factor productivity in Australia has been slow compared with other OECD countries, the evidence that we are not high up in the innovation stakes can be seen in indicators such as relative expenditure on R & D, relative importance of 'high tech' (R & D intensive) production and exports, the high tech trade balance, and Australian patent applications in foreign countries (EPAC Discussion Paper 91/08, pp. 7–9, 23–9). A report to the Prime Minister's Science Council showed that the nation's use of advanced machine tools and other manufacturing technology was much lower than in countries such as UK and Taiwan, and a Monash University study indicated that less than 3% of the nation's manufacturers use comprehensive quality management practices (*The Australian*, 9 June 1992).

Although there has been an encouraging trend in all these indicators in the second half of the 1980s, the basic problem remains. Barry Jones often reminds us that of 12 OECD countries surveyed, in 11 of them the fastest growing economic sector in the 1980s was computers and electronics whereas in Australia it was real estate.

So the conclusion is largely inescapable: we have not been a strong productivity performer and if we want to improve our material living standards at a faster rate than we have, we must focus our attention on the main factors driving productivity, such as capital per head (investment rate), technical progress, economies of scale, gains in resource allocation efficiency, improvements in the quality of work force (education and training), and the average rate of utilisation of capital (stability of economic environment, work practices etc.). A study has been commissioned by CEDA on this broad question.

2 The second performance criteria was *economic stability*. Here the full evidence has not yet been put together but a preliminary judgment can be made. If we limit our observations to the period up to the mid-1980s, the level of instability in Australia, measured in terms of standard deviation from trend, does not look too bad (Shann 1984, Kakwani 1991).

However, when the figures are updated to include our disastrous 1990–91 recession it appears we may have suffered from a relatively high and increasing degree of instability over the last two decades as a whole, and especially the 1980s. A preliminary analysis suggests that in the period 1982–92, Australia's standard deviation from the mean was higher than in any earlier post-war period, and higher than most European countries and Japan. Australia's 1990–91 recession was probably the fourth deepest of all the OECD countries, with only Finland, NZ, and UK performing worse than us on this criterion (*The Economist*, March 1992, p. 72). Further work is needed to confirm these impressions. A study has been commissioned by CEDA on Australia's relative stability experience.

The key factors determining the stability performance of an economy are: the structure of exportables and importables and hence the vulnerability of external trade to terms of trade shocks; the extent of wage and price flexibility in response to external shocks; the extent to which the economy is prone to internally generated shocks such as wage push or excess demand, especially for imports; the effectiveness of macroeconomic management; the stability and integrity of the financial system; and the fragility of corporate balance sheets.

On some of these—stability of the financial system, corporate balance sheets, macro wage flexibility—Australia probably compares reasonably well with other countries. The other factors will need attention if we want to achieve more stable growth in the future.

3 Our third performance test was *unemployment*. The story here is quite simple and quite dismal. Since the 1960s there has been a steady upward trend in the unemployment rate. In the 1960s the average unemployment rate averaged 1.7%; in the 1970s it averaged 4.5%; in the last decade it averaged 7.6%; and in 1991–92 (admittedly a year of recession) it will probably average close to 10%—the highest figure recorded in any post-war recession.

This is not a unique Australian phenomenon. Several OECD countries have also experienced a rising long term trend. However the rise in Australia has been particularly marked.

It is also significant that the incidence of 'hidden' unemployment has been showing a similar tendency to increase. The ABS recently reported a total under-utilisation rate of 15%, of which 5 percentage points was under-employment (people who do not work as many hours as they would like).

The number of long term unemployed has increased at a particularly alarming rate—from under 5% of the jobless pool in the late 1960s to between 1/5 and 1/3 of the jobless in the last few years. On reasonable assumptions about the timing and strength of the economic recovery, the number of long term unemployed is projected to reach 300 000 in 1994, compared with 190 000 in 1983 and around 50 000 in the mid-1970s (Chapman et al. 1992). The trend in long term unemployment normally mirrors the trend in aggregate unemployment but with a lag.

The upward break in aggregate unemployment in the 1970s has been largely attributed to the oil shocks and wage overhang (Castles 1992), but the continuance of the upward trend in the 1980s is harder to explain. In the last decade Australia had smaller real wage increases relative to productivty than most OECD countries (EPAC CP 47, p. 38).

The rise in aggregate unemployment in the 1980s can be apportioned into three parts. One part may have reflected a further *increase in the 'natural' unemployment rate*—the lowest rate consistent with low and non-accelerating inflation (Borland 1990), possibly caused by stickiness in wage *relativities* in the face of accelerated strucutural change, and by a deterioration in the unemployed workers' human capital in a generally difficult labour market. However the evidence is far from conclusive.

A second part of the rise in unemployment may have reflected an *intentional* decision of the authorities to give unemployment lower priority relative to other goals and to deliberately accept the risk that unemployment might thereby rise *above its natural rate*. This may have been due to concerns about trade union push (as in the early 1980s), or concerns about the balance of payments and external debt (as in the mid to late 1980s), or fears of an uncontrolled asset price boom (as in the late 1980s—see reported acknowledgment of this point by the Deputy Governor Ian McFarlane in *The Australian*, 22 May 1992).

A third part of the rise in unemployment was probably the *unintended* result of external shocks and mismanagement of these shocks.

A national economic strategy which sought to achieve a much better performance on the unemployment front would need to focus on these areas, especially the structural rigidities underlying the natural unemployment rate; the balance of payments constraint on growth; and the management of economic cycles and shocks.

4 The fourth suggested economic performance criterion was the *distribution of incomes and wealth*—which was used as a proxy for justice and fairness. Here too the full picture is not yet clear. A preliminary verdict is that inequality, as traditionally measured (e.g. using a Gini coefficient), significantly increased in Australia over the last two decades (Saunders 1989, Stilwell 1992), reversing a consistent trend towards equalisation over the previous 50 years (McLean in Maddock 1987, Berry 1987).

It also appears, on the sparse evidence available, that inequality may now be greater in Australia than in a large number of OECD countries, including Britain, Canada, Norway and Sweden (Smeeding 1988–89, Saunders 1990). This is despite an egalitarian wages system, a closely targetted social security system and relatively heavy reliance on progressive income taxes.

Caution is needed however in relying simply on measures such as the Gini coefficient in assessing income distribution, whether it be trends over time or levels across countries. In particular, strong growth in female and part-time employment and changes in the age composition of the work force can distort trends and comparisons. It is also clear that there has been a wide variation in the experience of families, with single-income couples with dependents having suffered relative to couples without dependents (Bradbury 1990). As well, international comparisons are fraught with problems of data comparability.

There is, however, some corroborative evidence of growing inequality from another source—trends in wage distribution. A recent study has found evidence that increasing numbers of male middle-income workers have been joining the ranks of low-paid workers and that wage differentials between high and low paid jobs have been widening (Professor Bob Gregory in unpublished paper 1992).

In addition, inequality has been boosted by the recent trend towards higher unemployment. We have already noted that the situation of the long term unemployed has deteriorated; and unemployment among non-English speaking migrants has become quite alarming.

It also appears that in Australia, as in Canada, regional disparities in income and employment have tended to increase (EPAC CP 46).

While therefore any verdict in this area must be a highly qualified one, it appears on the surface that there may have been an underlying trend towards higher income inequality in the last couple of decades, and that this has been more marked than in many other countries. Further research has been commissioned by CEDA on this question.

The picture is not however all gloomy. Reflecting the large and consistent increases in expenditure on Aboriginal programs, it seems that the relative incomes of Aborigines have increased (Gruen and Grattan in unpublished paper 1992), although their employment, health, housing and educational disabilities are still enormous (see articles in *The Australian*, 27 May 1992).

Again, it appears that the poorest 10% of the population have probably improved their relative lot in the 1980s. Family and child poverty, which reached a high level by the mid-1980s, was specifically targetted by the Hawke Government's family allowance supplement and appears to have fallen considerably over the period 1983/84 to 1989/90 (Bradbury 1990 and 1991). While people at the top increased their income share, this was at the expense of middle income families rather than of the poor. So on one important dimension of our social performance—the poverty gap—the results are rather more reassuring.

As to the distribution of wealth in Australia, the available information is scarce and uncertain. We know that (if one excludes housing, where wider home ownership and rising house prices may have had a 'levelling effect') the share of net wealth held by the very rich (the *BRW* 'Rich' list) increased appreciably during the 1980s (Stilwell 1992); by contrast, relative wealth shares remained fairly stable in the previous 50 years (McLean 1987, Berry 1987). However, apart from the poor quality of the data, the timing of the studies may have a bearing on the results; given the volatile changes in relative wealth over the last few years, a review of the *BRW* 'Rich' today might produce different results.

What is clear is that personal wealth in Australia is heavily concentrated (the wealthiest 10% of income units holding 55% of total wealth) and that the tax system has tended to accentuate wealth inequalities (Dilnot AER 1990, Stilwell 1992).

5 Our fifth performance test was *quality of life*. This is the hardest of all to pass judgment on, and we hope to assemble some hard evidence as the work proceeds. The impression at this stage of the analysis is that the picture is a mixed one. On the one hand, the water we drink and bathe in may have become more polluted, our cities noisier, more congested and less safe, and our hospitals, education institutions and prisons more crowded.

However, we have made much progress on most other quality of life criteria such as health (e.g. life expectancy), education opportunities and participation rates, leisure, air pollution, quality and variety of goods and service on offer, standard of housing, speed of communication, and most importantly, genuine equality of opportunity (it is easy to forget that as recently as the 1950s or early 1960s there was open and blatant discrimination against Aborigines, women and non-Anglo migrants).

What is also fairly clear is that on most of the above criteria, as well as others such as literacy, individual liberty, political stability, availability of outdoor recreation space, commuting time, safety in the streets etc., our quality of life is still very high compared with that of most other countries (EPAC BP No. 10, p. 166, United Nations Human Development report 1992, and I. Castles 1992).

Nonetheless, the Minister for Arts, Sport, the Environment and Territories, Ros Kelly, recently reminded us that, although in Australia we are sheltered from a range of environmental problems experienced in the northern hemisphere, such as acid rain, contaminated food and drinking water, we have problems of our own: 'particularly in our urban areas, ozone and other photochemical pollutants exceed internationally recognised health guidelines. We are all too well aware of the problems of Sydney's beaches and of recent problems with toxic algae in our water ways, chemical pollution and turbidity, salinity…' (Speech 9/4/92).

Nor can we afford to be complacent about the implications for our economic sovereignty of continuing to rely heavily on foreign saving to finance our investment needs. B.A. Santamaria was being more than a bit melodramatic when he said recently that 'Australia has already forfeited its economic sovereignty…and without economic independence, political independence does not exist' (*The Australian*, 7–8 March 1992), but we should heed the warning signs.

6 Turning to the sixth and final performance test—*inter-generational equity*, measured in terms of net wealth accumulated and bequeathed to future Australians—the story is not as positive as some may think.

Certainly, if one takes a very narrow view of net wealth, measuring it in terms of private fixed capital, such as dwellings, household durables, and business assets, the picture looks fairly bright. On that definition, the private sector's real wealth per capita was some 50% higher at the end of the 1980s than at the end of the 1960s (Treasury 1990, Callen 1991, EPAC CP 40).

However, this offers an incomplete measure of the overall wealth bequeathed to future Australians—for a number of reasons.

First, it is not clear that the Australian education system is 'doing right for our children': our school children may not be tested, challenged and stretched as fully as their counterparts in countries such as Germany (see, for example, L.Chadderton in *The Canberra Times*, 10 June 1992). In other words, our stock of human capital may not be growing as impressively as our stock of houses, hotels and factories.

Second, it appears that the net wealth of the public sector, unlike that of the private sector, has not increased in the last two decades and may actually have declined. The OECD recently studied the balance sheets of governments in the US, Japan, Germany, France, the UK, Italy and Canada, and found that in the last decade, general government net worth (government fixed stock less financial liabilities) declined markedly in every country studied except Japan. This has happened because public debt has grown faster than the capital stock (Chouraqui et al. 1986).

While comparable figures are not available for Australia, we know that in this country (1) there was a relatively sharp decline in general government investment in the decade 1970 to 1990 (*The Economist*, 25 January 1992); and (2) net public debt as a percentage of GDP grew relatively strongly until the mid-1980s (EPAC CP 44, p. 22). So it is likely that a similar decline in general government net wealth would have occurred in Australia in the period studied by the OECD.

Some recent preliminary estimates by EPAC of public sector fixed assets at replacement prices tend to broadly confirm this impression—which is hardly surprising given the severe budgetary constraints for many years, and the disproportionate share of the restraint burden borne by capital spending (EPAC CP 49).

If a decline in public sector net wealth has indeed occurred over the last two decades this is not (at least in the absence of closer analysis) necessarily a cause for concern; but it must be set against the gains in private net wealth noted earlier.

A third reason why we need to look beyond the apparent rise in private sector wealth is that traditional measures of private sector net wealth only take account of what has happened to human-made or physical capital and ignore *natural capital*. And it is in the area of natural capital that we have been most neglectful of the interests of future generations.

Conventional national accounts record changes in wealth only when they pass through the market. They do not allow for depletion of non-renewable resources: when we cut down a forest and the product is sold, the national accounts show an increase in output of forest products and implicitly an increase in wealth. Yet if the trees are not replaced, we are in effect drawing down our natural capital; in addition we are enhancing the risk of soil erosion, flooding, loss of agricultural productivity etc.

We are frequently reminded of the damage done to our natural environment over the last few decades and much evidence has been collected by the CSIRO, the Department of Arts, Sport, the Environment & Territories, and more recently by the Australian Bureau of Statistics (*Australia's Environment: Issues and Facts*). On the basis of this evidence there are claims that more than half our arid and semi-arid land, which supports much of our agricultural and pastoral industries, is significantly degraded, and estimates of the losses to agriculture from the impact of land degradation in the Murray–Darling Basin alone exceed $200 million a year (speech by Ros Kelly, Minister for the Arts, Sport, the Environment & Territories, 9 April 1992). There are also claims of extensive deforestation, and irreparable damage to both freshwater and marine environments, with major loss of biological diversity. It is said that all NSW inland rivers are now so polluted that they are unfit even for farm animals to drink from (Nature Conservation Council, Australia, 11 January 1992). Almost one in five of Australia's 20 000 known species of plants are either rare or threatened.

We have seen the accumulation of carbon dioxide and other trace gases in the global atmosphere with unpredictable and potentially very harmful implications for climate; Australia is said to produce more greenhouse gases per capita than citizens of almost any other nation, and carbon dioxide gas emissions per capita appear to have increased appreciably between 1971 and 1988. We have also seen a rapid accumulation of solid and hazardous waste, causing widespread concern and putting Australia among the worst offenders per capita in the world league. We have allowed over-use of chemicals to severely damage the ozone layer.

'The losses appear quite staggering. And that is not just an episode in our colonial past—it is still happening today' (Ros Kelly, ibid.).

Many believe these claims are over-alarmist and often based on questionable evidence; they also point to offsetting human-made improvements in pasture and soil quality from the application of capital and technology, reforestation programs, mining rehabilitation programs etc. They also deny that our environmental record is uniformly dismal: for example, kangaroo numbers have increased over the last decade, and the percentage of Australia's land covered by native forests has barely decreased and that of rainforest has increased (see McGuinness in *The Australian*, 3 June 1992).

Nonetheless the evidence is sufficient to make all Australians pause and think about the implications for future generations if environmental damage were to continue at the same pace as in the past.

There is a fourth and final reason why we cannot merely look at private human-made wealth when assessing whether we have been fair to future Australians. We need to also examine the possibility that we 'saved too little', 'invested in the wrong things', and 'drew too heavily on overseas savings'.

Our gross domestic saving fell from a range of about 24% to 26% of GDP in the 1950s, 1960s and early 1970s, to a range of about 19 to 21% thereafter (but note that some recovery was evident in the second half of the 1980s; note also that when adjusted for the holding gains and losses on financial assets from inflation, the long term trend in gross private saving appears to have been fairly stable—(Edey and Britten-Jones 1990)).

This apparent 'decline' in saving proves nothing in itself. The argument that we have saved too little, in terms of our obligations to future generations, rests essentially on two arguable, although essentially unverifiable, propositions:

a that Australian governments, like many other OECD governments, may not have saved enough in the last two decades to maintain adequate infrastructure investment, and in that sense may have under-provided for future generations; public concerns about the deteriorating state of our infrastructure, while often greatly exaggerated, do have a degree of justification, as various EPAC reports have shown (Council Papers 33, 43, 44); and

b that, because of tax and inflationary distortions or because of myopia and over-optimistic expectations, Australians may have put too little value on future consumption, and the well-being of future Australians, relative to current consumption (although this could now be changing), and may have relied excessively on debt to finance their investment needs in the 1980s.

An argument can also be made that too often we have invested in the wrong things i.e. too much of our investment has gone into relatively unproductive assets. This proposition has several legs to it: that we allowed too much of our scarce capital to be channelled into highly protected industries (TCF, motor vehicles, chemicals) which have not proved viable in the long run; that our investment in exportables has been low by world standards; that, in the poorly regulated, speculative and inflationary environment of the 1980s, credit and investment standards were allowed to degenerate, and many households and businesses made investment decisions which were basically uneconomic; that the tax system was biased against plant and equipment relative to real estate, and against assets with a relatively long effective life comparative to shorter term assets (Freebairn, EPAC 1990 and 'Government Business Tax Review', reported in *Australian Financial Review*, 12 February 1992); that rigid work practices prevented plant from being used to its maximum potential; and finally that our system of Government has inhibited national priority setting and contributed to a misallocation of capital in the public sector (EPAC Council Paper No. 33).

It is significant that the average 'productivity' of capital in Australia (the inverse of the capital output ratio) was significantly lower at the end of the 1980s than at the start of the 1970s (although an improvement in the trend was apparent during the 1980s); moreover, while international comparisons in this area must be treated with great caution, average productivity for the business sector as a whole and for many individual sectors appears to be appreciably lower in Australia than in other developed countries (EPAC Council Paper No. 43, pp. 17 and 18; and EPAC Research Paper No. 1, May 1992, p. 11), although the relative gap may be narrowing.

It is also significant that until very recently our export performance was bad (Banks 1990), and that the overall size of our traded goods sector declined from over 25% in the early 1970s to only 22% or so in the late 1980s (Dwyer 1991)—suggesting again some misallocation of resources in Australia.

As will be pointed out later, many of our capital inefficiency and misallocation problems have been corrected. But much of the damage has been done as far as future populations are concerned. Reflecting our low propensity to save relative to our investment needs, and the relatively low returns on investment, our net external debt increased from under 5% at the start of the 1970s to over 33% by the end of the 1980s; and net investment income payable abroad rose from around 1.5% of GDP at the start of the 1970s to over 4% of GDP by the end of the 1980s (although, with lower interest rates, this has since tended to decline).

While there are clearly different opinions within the economics profession on both the seriousness of this problem and its policy implications, it is the view of the writer that the large debt hangover at the start of the 1990s is likely to increase our vulnerability to shocks and constrain our economic growth in future years, unless we can quickly stabilise the trend.

To sum up the record on inter-generational equity: our stock of private wealth (houses, factories, equipment, hotels etc.) has probably grown in line with or faster than GDP, but the evidence on human capital, public capital, natural capital and on our external liabilities is much less reassuring.

In brief, looking back over the past 20 years, what should be the verdict on the performance of the Australian economy?

It is of course very difficult for a country to perform well on all the six tests we have laid down. To an extent, countries deliberately choose to trade one set of goals against another. For example, the so-called Asian tigers have achieved something close to an economic miracle over the last decade—with strong and relatively stable per capita growth and rising employment—but they have chosen to live with a high degree of social inequality, poor living conditions, relatively undemocratic institutions and a considerable degradation of the environment.

However, Australia's bad performance on the three key economic criteria—per capita growth, stability and unemployment—cannot be explained in terms of a desire to enhance social equity, quality of life or the environment, as even in these three latter respects the record is patchy and in parts worrying.

Nor can our low per capita growth be simply explained in terms of 'catch up' by nations with lower living standards than Australia. Professor Gruen's comment a few years ago (Gruen 1986) that 'we have performed less well than one would expect purely on the basis of our high real income at the beginning' is still pertinent today—perhaps more so.

It should be stressed that this gloomy assessment relates to the experience of the past twenty years as revealed in the statistical data. As we note later, important steps have been and are still being taken to address our problems and these are laying the seed for a markedly improved performance in the decades ahead.

CHAPTER

3

FACTORS BEARING ON OUR POOR ECONOMIC PERFORMANCE

The next step in developing a long term strategy is to assess why we went wrong. Specificially, why has the economy under-performed over the last twenty years, in terms of per capita growth, stability and unemployment?

We have already hinted at many of the immediate causes. We know that we saved and exported too little, borrowed too much, produced too little relative to our resources, paid ourselves too much relative to our productivity and performance (with inflationary consequences), invested too little (relative to our population growth) and in the wrong places, under-utilised our capital stock for long periods, and failed to innovate and improve our human capital at the same rate as our competitors. But these are symptoms rather than causes. We need to look behind them at the underlying forces at work.

Many studies have sought to identify the factors which have adversely affected one or more dimension of our economic performance (see, for example, Kasper et al. 1980, Maddock & McLean 1987, Gruen 1986, V. Argy 1992, and numerous papers by the Industry Commission, BIE, and EPAC). These underlying factors can usefully be grouped under seven headings: institutional barriers; attitudinal constraints; an unpropitious tax/price incentive climate; market failure; adverse external influences; failures of macroeconomic policy; and high population growth.

(i)
Institutional barriers

The institutions which might have held back our economic performance include the federal system, the industrial relations system, our system of education and training, and the relative strength of narrowly based sectional interests in our political processes.

Australians generally favour preservation of a *federal system* because it offers them a greater degree of regional, political and social diversity and autonomy. Ideally however they would also like to retain most of the benefits of economic integration—coordination, harmonisation, free flow of trade and resources, cohesive and consistent national standards. Instead, we have seen unnecessary duplication, overlap and entanglement of functional responsibilities, and disharmony of regulations, leading to wastage, policy delays and confusion, and high business compliance costs (EPAC 1990).

Concerns have also been expressed about our system of *education and training*. Not only does it appear that we may have under-invested in human capital overall (Gruen 1986, OECD economic survey of Australia 1992), but there are doubts about the effectiveness of some of this investment.

Our education system has not produced people with adequate literacy, numeracy and communication skills, and it has not produced the trade, professional and management skills required by Australian industry. In particular, engineers and scientists have been emerging from our universities with inadequate training in business practice, management and accounting or an entrepreneurial spirit. Conversely, many of our managerial executives appear to lack the necessary scientific and technical skills and know-how.

In its recent economic survey of Australia (1992), the OECD contends that our system of education and training has not kept up with increases in educational attainment overseas, has been biased against vocational skills, and has produced skilled workers that are trained too narrowly (see also *Australian Financial Review* editorial, 15 June 1992).

There is still no nationally consistent framework for the recognition of education qualifications and training competence. We have been slow to exploit the opportunities to build up a major education export industry with Asia. Our universities have had to contend with over-crowding, unmet demand, and for a time, insufficiently competitive remuneration to attract high quality teaching staff. Industry has invested far too little in in-house training, and its contribution has been too cyclical in character.

The *industrial relations system* can be assessed in terms of four criteria: first, its effect on the stability of the macroeconomic environment; second, its effect on resource allocation efficiency; third, the implications of the system for social equity; and finally its impact on work place efficiency, flexibility and more generally on the adaptability and innovativeness of Australian enterprises.

It can be argued that—at least over the last ten years—our centralised system of conciliation and arbitration has generally served Australia well on the first three counts—it has almost certainly produced lower aggregate wage outcomes at any given level of trade union power and labour demand pressures (Chapman 1991); the relative uniformity of wages relative to work value has ensured that labour is paid everywhere its opportunity cost, which is a key requirement for resource allocation efficiency (Isaac 1988); and the centralist system has produced a more egalitarian wage structure and helped to protect vulnerable workers from exploitation (Mulvey 1986, Norris 1986).

However, our industrial relations system has failed us on the last count: it has been slow to adjust to the growing need for work place flexibility and speed of response in an increasingly specialised, integrated and competitive world market. In that sense, the industrial relations system must carry a fair share of the blame for the lack of dynamic competitiveness of the Australian economy.

The final institutional constraint on economic growth has been the *structure and strength of organised pressure groups*. Interest groups have tended to be narrowly based and have been able to exercise considerable influence by taking advantage of the Federal division of powers, the existence of often hostile upper chambers, the frequency of elections, the closely competitive positions of the two political parties, and the lack of anything approaching national consensus on most key policy issues.

They have used democratic institutions to preserve the status quo and delay reform (as with protection and trade union featherbedding practices).

Indeed it has been argued (e.g. Mancur Olsen, cited in Keating & Dixon 1989) that Australia's low per capita growth in the 1970s and early 1980s was a reflection of the strength of organised labour and of the protectionist lobby. More recently the influence of the greenies may have at times been unnecessarily inhibiting for economic growth, although full credit must be given to them for contributing to a much-needed transformation in public attitudes to the environment.

(ii) Attitudinal constraints

The attitudinal problem is to be found in the work place—a 'them and I' attitude, a tendency for unions to resist technological change and protect inefficient practices and rigidities, and for management to look for the course of least resistance. There was also a tendency for Australian business to look inwardly rather than globally, to focus principally on Europe rather than Asia, and to expect and demand too much from government: in a recent Monash University survey, 2/3 of companies believed they should receive government subsidies, grants or promotion assistance to adopt the best quality management practices of their competitors! (*The Australian*, 8 June 1992).

(iii) The incentive climate provided by governments

In a private enterprise system, decisions to save, work, invest and export are in large part determined by the incentive climate i.e. relative prices and rewards. This climate in turn is heavily influenced by government pricing policies, the structure of taxation and social benefits, trade policy and regulation.

All of these have been sending out perverse signals over the greater part of the last twenty years: to borrow and consume rather than save or invest; to invest short rather than long; to invest in real estate rather than industrial plant and equipment; to draw on the available pool of overseas and local skills rather than train or retrain; to invest in sheltered sections of the domestic market rather than in traded goods sectors; to over-produce in some areas; to opt for leisure rather than work; to stay on welfare benefits rather than go out to work; and (at least until recently) to over-exploit rather than conserve certain natural resources.

Thus, as noted earlier, the tax system may have been partly responsible for the splurge on relatively unproductive property in the 1980s (McKibbon 1991, Freebairn 1990); trade policies were responsible for wasteful investments in over-protected industries that proved non-viable in the long run, such as TCF, motor vehicles, chemicals; unsound government pricing policies and poor co-ordination between public authorities were responsible for over-capitalisation of certain public services such as rural roads and electricity (EPAC CP 33 and CP 43) and for over-exploitation of natural resources such as native saw logs, fisheries, water and energy (EPAC BP 16); lack of effective prudential regulation contributed to the destabilising debt splurge of the 1980s (EPAC BP 14); over-regulation of the wage structure was at least partly responsible for rigidities in the work place and for the general tendency for industry to under-invest in training; over-regulation of rural industries contributed to inefficient production of eggs and dairy products and to the build-up of stocks of wool (the wool reserve scheme); some ambiguity and instability in environmental regulation and policy increased the risks associated with mineral development; and under-regulation of companies and securities and financial institutions contributed to the instability of the late 1980s.

(iv)
Market imperfections

Market imperfections and limitations have also contributed to our poor economic performance.

Markets do not always produce economically efficient or desirable outcomes, measured in terms of social net benefits. This can arise because of externalities, public goods, and natural monopolies. Governments everywhere have recognised such market failures and have intervened in education, health, the provision of essential public services, regulation of the environment, management of the economy, etc. although as we note in various parts of this report, they have not always intervened effectively or efficiently in these areas.

The issue we are addressing here, however, relates to market imperfections arising from information deficiencies, inadequate competition, myopia, or misperception of risk. These have shown up in several areas.

First, the assumption that, left to the market, exchange rates would always tend to move in an equilibrating manner and in line with fundamentals (such as productivity, competitiveness and the terms of trade) has not been borne out in practice. The market has been greatly influenced by short term interest rate relativities and short term exchange rate expectations, and there is some evidence of speculative inefficiency (EPAC BP 9, V. Argy 1992, p. 236). As a result it is arguable that for much of the 1980s the Australian dollar, although possibly under-valued in terms of purchasing power, was over-valued relative to what was needed in the long run to stabilise our external debt situation (F. Argy 1991).

This exchange rate over-valuation coincided with a freeing up of our import trade barriers, so that the combined effect was to seriously erode the relative incentive to invest in the traded goods sector, measured in terms of the prices of exportables and importables relative to prices of non-traded goods and services (EPAC CP 47, pp. 8–10).

This does not mean however that the Hawke Government was at fault in floating the exchange rate. There was no way any government could have successfully maintained capital controls and manipulated the exchange rate at will after the mid-1980s even if it wanted to. And, given the dominance of terms of trade shocks, flexible exhange rates almost certainly helped to insulate the Australian economy against external disturbances (V. Argy 1992). In any case, periods of over-valuation of the dollar were partly due to relatively high interest rates, which were at least in part a fault of economic management (White 1992).

A second example of market imperfection was in credit markets following financial deregulation. The behaviour of many banks and other financial institutions was imprudent and ill-judged even in purely commercial terms. This behaviour was greatly facilitated by what (at least in retrospect) was clearly an over-accommodating monetary policy and by a failure on the part of the Government to match bank lending and interest rate deregulation with adequate prudential regulation or supervision (as envisaged by the Campbell Committee in its 1982 report).

However, as the *Australian Financial Review* put it recently in an editorial (20 March 1992), 'the Federal Government handed the banks the gun during the 1980s...but it was the banks that pulled the trigger by lending too much too often on little security'. The result—a rise in both residential and commercial property prices of about 50% between 1987 and 1989 (Callen 1991, Treasury 1990)—was a classic 'speculative bubble' founded on false hopes and unrealistic expectations. It was a case where the Government was excessively trusting of the market.

Third, it can be argued that the conditions for an efficient, competitive market were lacking in Australia for most of the period under study. This was in part because of high protection levels but equally it was due to a number of other factors: there were unnecessary regulatory constraints on competition in many key areas of transport such as airlines, rail, shipping and stevedoring, and in power and communications (IC 1991, and relevant reports); there was a failure to properly regulate natural monopolies to ensure they did not abuse their market power (IC 1991); and there was no effective competition policy in place for much of the private sector of the economy: in particular Australia has accepted levels of industry concentration (e.g. in sections of transport, building materials and retailing) and anti-competitive practices (e.g. in the building industry and the professions) that would not be tolerated in the USA. Deficiencies in competition were recently underlined in the report of the Royal Commission into the NSW Building Industry, which revealed widespread 'price fixing, collusive tendering and other trade malpractices by employers, as well as trade union abuses' (*The Australian*, 28 May 1992).

The absence of strong domestic competition may have blunted the incentive to efficiency and innovation and left Australian industry ill-prepared for the cold winds of world competition.

To achieve maximum benefits for innovation, competition may need to be tempered by cooperative arrangements such as a mechanism for firms to share the financing and diffusion of scientific research; moreover competition alone is not enough to ensure successful innovation: it is important also to have a strong scientific and research base and educational system and receptive, sophisticated domestic consumers. Nonetheless, a domestic industrial structure exposed to intense competition is a critical ingredient in dynamic competitiveness (*The Economist*, 11 January 1992).

Fourth, there is a concern (one not unique to Australia and at this stage not fully substantiated) that markets have tended to assess performance in too short term a time horizon. In particular it is argued that investment advisers and the media have tended to report on and evaluate the performance of fund managers on the basis of their short term results, and over-geared or under-valued corporations have sought to nurture their cash flows and look for early returns to deter potential takeover aspirants. The tax system in Australia may also have discouraged longer term investment (as noted earlier) and further compounded the effects of market myopia.

The overall effect may have been to deter technological innovations or investments where the returns were considered long term and uncertain. Similar concerns have been expressed in other anglo-saxon countries, e.g. the US Competitiveness Council established by Congress cited as one of the underlying causes of the USA's competitiveness problem that 'the private and public sector in the United States tend to think and act with a short term horizon' (media release, 4 March 1992).

Finally, the market left to itself has in the past arguably failed to give enough weight to the interests of future generations, especially in regard to the environment. Markets cannot be expected to take account of social externalities: it is up to governments to ensure the incentive climate is right (see discussion above). However many of the concerns about land degradation—one of the most serious environmental and resource problems facing Australia—relate to land in private ownership and reflect poor land management practices (EPAC BP 16).

Many of the market failures instanced above, such as the occasional bouts of exchange rate disequilibrium and asset price speculation, were not of course peculiar to Australia and cannot explain per se our relatively poor economic performance in international terms. However, some, such as the level of domestic competition, were more pervasive in Australia. More importantly, our external account imbalance made us rather more vulnerable to the effects of the market failures.

The mere existence of market failure is not of course a sufficient justification per se for government intervention. There are costs, many of them unintended, in government intervention. 'Government failure' is no less common than market failure and can arise from a variety of causes, some of them inherent in any democracy (such as ambiguous mandates, rent-seeking lobbyists, pork barrelling, limited time horizons induced by electoral cycles), and others arising from public service inflexibilities and remoteness from the market place, excessive requirements for public accountability, diffusion of authority, especially in a federal system, absence of vigorous competition and so on.

Government intervention to correct for market failure is only justified if governments have superior information or skills and cannot impart these to the market, and only after every effort has been made to correct the underlying problem, such as unnecessary barriers to competition. And where intervention is justified, it is important to ensure that instruments of intervention are used which make as much use of the market as possible, so as to minimise by-product distortions. This issue is taken up again in a later chapter.

(v) External factors

External factors beyond our control have undoubtedly contributed to our poor economic performance in the last twenty years: in particular, we have suffered from an underlying decline and instability in our commodity export prices and from foreign trade restrictions and subsidies in some important agricultural markets. These were important factors in our poor export performance (Banks 1991). As well, the offer of competitive investment concessions by other net capital importers may have diverted possible investment capital from Australia.

There is not much we could have done about these problems—apart from exerting whatever influence we could in international forums. It would not have been sensible to try to match every individual export and investment subsidy offered by another country; unless we were sure that the foreign subsidy was only going to be temporary in duration, a reciprocal response by Australia would simply have had the effect of improving the living standards of foreigners in third countries at the expense of Australian consumers or taxpayers. In any case most of our competitors have deeper pockets than we have and we would most likely have come out second best in any subsidy war.

We could have offered across the board incentives to manufacturing and service industries with the aim of diversifying our industrial base and pattern of trade. This would have made our exportables and importables more alike, and thus reduced our exposure to terms of trade disturbances. But while this would have enhanced the stability of the economy, it would probably have been at the cost of lower average living standards (Makin 1992).

The issue of what role governments might play in industry development in the future is raised later in this paper.

(vi)
Failures of macroeconomic policy

In the past twenty years governments have made a number of costly errors in macro policy and these have contributed to the volatility and relatively slow growth of per capita incomes. (For a fuller account see V. Argy 1992.)

The Whitlam years (1972–75) saw major social reforms, the first major steps towards a more open, competitive economy and the start of the process of greater integration with Asia; but in macroeconomic management the big failures were wage policy, which operated in a perverse manner, and monetary policy, which was too volatile.

The Fraser governments made some progress towards structural fiscal balance but then blew much of it away at the end. While an attempt was made to maintain stable monetary conditions, there was little evidence of a coherent monetary policy directed at long term objectives such as inflation. Wage policy was erratic—too confrontationist at times and too accommodating at others; and swinging from extreme free market bargaining policies to highly centralist ones.

The Hawke/Keating governments introduced fundamental tax reforms which helped to broaden the tax base and improve tax neutrality. They also contributed to a transformation in public attitudes on efficiency, Asia, and industrial relations, created a far more open economy than the one they inherited in 1983, introduced wide ranging microeconomic reforms etc. (see later) and generally 'got the big strategic decisions right' (*The Economist*, 4 April 1992).

However their macroeconomic management performance was quite patchy. A major strength was wage policy—much maligned for its microeconomic effects but arguably effective in maintaining aggregate wage restraint (Chapman 1991), especially in the difficult period after devaluation in the mid-1980s. Fiscal policy, after a slow start which initially contributed to the current account deficit, was also generally sound from a long term structural viewpoint.

Nonetheless mistakes were clearly made (V. Argy 1992, Garry White 1991, Walsh 1991, Pitchford 1992):

- a critical macro policy failure in the last 10 years or so was that governments were slow to read and react to the economic indicators—a failure which probably had little or nothing to do with Canberra's 'isolation', since most business economists closely in touch with the market failed just as spectacularly to forecast short term developments;
- such deficiencies were compounded by the difficulties in predicting policy impacts and lags in the new environment of financial deregulation; in these circumstances it is not surprising that too much was expected of short term economic management and too little achieved: indeed the results were perverse at times (policy was too permissive in 1987–88 because of exaggerated concern about the likely flow-on damage from the October 1987 stock market crash; and it was excessively restrictive in 1990–91 long after the decline had started);
- while recognising that governments are constrained by public attitudes (e.g. to taxes), there was a tendency, especially after 1988, to rely excessively on monetary policy (relative to fiscal, wages and structural policy) to achieve any given inflation/current account deficit outcome—with undesirable effects on the exchange rate and the mix of consumption and investment;
- it can be argued that, apart from the monetary/fiscal mix, more could have been done through 'jawboning' and the provision of

information to influence long run expectations in foreign exchange markets: while the use of monetary policy to target the exchange rate has little support amongst economists (Argy 1992, ch. 24), there is possibly a little scope for high profile 'sterilised' intervention to influence the exchange rate and this could have been used at times when, in the opinion of the authorities, the market was palpably out of line with long run fundamentals;

- there was at times an unfortunate ambiguity in the Government's macroeconomic policy rhetoric; the Government should have done more to dampen the community's income and asset price expectations in the second half of the 1980s, and it should have more publicly and forcefully announced it was tightening monetary policy in 1988–89, so as to speed up its impact;
- one can point to the failure to match the fast pace of banking and exchange control deregulation in the early 1980s with adequate prudential regulation and supervision;
- the decision to increase the immigration intake in the mid-1980s probably aggravated our balance of payments problems in the subsequent years; and
- capital expenditure cuts bore a disproportionate share of the fiscal adjustment after 1983–84, with implications noted earlier.

(vii) Population growth

Apart from the possibility that *increases* in immigration may have impeded macroeconomic management in the 1980s, it has been argued more generally that high population growth (the second highest in the OECD) was a factor holding down per capita growth in Australia in the late 1970s and 1980s. (See, for example, Gruen 1986, and Maddock & McLean 1987.) This is still a matter of debate among economists (see Nevile 1991 and associated articles by Withers and Parmenter, as well as various studies for the Bureau of Immigration Research); but it is at least arguable that immigration impacted adversely through one of two channels.

If it is assumed that the *investment rate did not increase* in response to higher population growth (and the evidence is unclear on this issue), then it could be argued that immigration produced a lower stock of capital per head than would otherwise be the case; this in turn would have tended to lower productivity—unless (as many e.g. Nevile argue) there were offsetting efficiency benefits from immigration (such as faster technological progress, scale economies, or a more flexible labour force). It should be noted that even if immigration did drive down GDP per head, the *incumbent* population may still have been better off on average as a result of immigration, although with a significant redistribution away from workers towards rentiers (Parmenter et al. 1991).

If on the other hand we were to assume that immigration *induced a rise in the investment rate* sufficient to maintain the trend in capital per head, then one could argue that immigration worsened our structural current account deficit, i.e. the trade-off between full employment GDP and external balance (Milbourne 1991, F. Argy 1990), with possible adverse effects on our growth performance—unless there were offsetting positive effects on savings and competitiveness e.g. through lower real wages.

The truth is we do not know what would have been an economically optimum overall immigration intake in the last two decades, but the possibility that immigration contributed to our poor economic performance in that period cannot be ruled out.

Acceptance of this possibility—and it is no more than a hypothesis—would not necessarily imply that continued high immigration in the 1970s and 1980s was a mistake (although there is little doubt that the increase in the mid-1980s was unwise). A full evaluation would have to take account of other possible effects of immigration on community well-being. These would include, for example, the gains in cultural diversity, national security (even if the gain in security were only perceived by a large section of the population) and international influence (which is as much a product of aggregate economics as of military power), and (on the negative side) possible harmful effects on the environment.

Apart from the question of what might have been an appropriate aggregate intake in the 1970s and 1980s, it can be argued that we should have altered the skill composition of the immigration program in a way which would have been more helpful to the economy (on this see, for example, Alan Wood, *The Australian*, 7 April 1992).

Whatever the merits of the respective arguments, it is opportune that both Government and Opposition are reviewing critically the net benefits of immigration, both its level and composition.

Are the problems being addressed?

This completes our brief review of the factors which might have had some bearing on our relatively poor economic performance in the last two decades.

It would be wrong to leave the reader with a wholly negative impression of our economic performance over the past twenty years. Some very encouraging changes have occurred in the 1980s which have not yet borne fruit but should impact very positively over the next decade. Indeed the 1960s can be viewed as a decade of strong growth in prosperity but where the seeds of economic decline were sowed, while the 1980s can be viewed as a decade of relatively poor economic outcomes but where the seeds of a future economic renaissance were laid.

In particular, a number of developments in the 1980s—not all welcome at the time—have helped to create an increased awareness and understanding of Australia's economic deficiencies and a climate more conducive to change. These developments include: major shocks to the Australian economy (wage explosions, terms of trade collapses, periodic crises in financial and foreign exchange markets and severe recessions); the opening up of the Australian economy to international competitive pressures and influence (partly as a consequence of the deregulation of the financial system and in more recent years the prospect of reduced protection); the increased strength of 'encompassing' interest groups relative to more narrowly-based sectional groups (an issue discussed further later); the corporate and financial excesses of the 1980s and the backlash that flowed from them; and the emergence of a more positive intellectual climate in the community: many formerly deeply contested issues, such as the relationship between wages and employment, the effects of protection, or the impact of expansionary fiscal policies, became the subject of near-consensus.

This more favourable climate assisted the Hawke/Keating governments to introduce many wide-ranging reforms. More importantly it contributed to a radical change in the attitudes and perceptions of trade unions and managers.

As a result, we saw major improvements in investment, labour market and public sector efficiency, signs of a break-through in export orientation, and a critical re-appraisal of macroeconomic policy.

Many of our investment efficiency problems have been corrected. In particular the tax system is more neutral, inflation is lower, tighter Stock Exchange and corporate standards are in place, financial institutions have moved up the learning curve of deregulation, increased work place flexibility is allowing better use of capital, and reduced protection and a slightly lower real exchange rate are encouraging a re-orientation towards internationally competitive industries.

Labour efficiency problems are being addressed through labour market reform, with greatly increased scope for work place bargaining, closer links between wages and productivity, and more flexibility in the deployment of labour at the enterprise level. The results are showing up quite dramatically in some areas such as in the waterfront, shipping, airlines, rail (Keating 1992), as well as in some sections of manufacturing (EPAC CP 45).

There have also been important gains in education participation rates (with the proportion of children who complete 12 years of schooling doubling from 35% to 70% and still rising), and an increased orientation of training and education towards the needs of the labour market.

Important steps have been or are being taken to transform the efficiency of the public sector. This includes: a rationalisation of the federal system e.g. through harmonisation of regulations, the establishment of a national electricity grid etc.; more rational pricing policies in regard to public services and natural resources; corporatisation of government business enterprises, with emphasis on bottom line performance and increased competition, leading to some dramatic results for productivity (EPAC CP 44, Keating 1992); increased efficiency in the public service (Department of Finance estimates of productivity growth in the Commonwealth public service are discussed in ABS 1992); greater use of tendering for public projects and greater application of cost-benefit analysis (e.g. in roads).

In the macroeconomic area, lessons have been painfully learnt from the experience with deregulation, asset inflation and the failures of short term economic management. One can reasonably expect a more stable and medium term oriented monetary stance in the future, directed more at the maintenance of low inflation, and a fiscal policy basically directed at structural external and internal balance but with sensitivity to short term economic fluctuations. The unknown at this stage is wage policy, but it is difficult to see us going backwards in this area.

The improved climate for change has produced a more outward orientation in Australian business culture. This is reflected in recent trends in manufacturing exports which cannot be wholly explained in terms of the recession. It is also reflected in an increasing tendency to see Australia as competing in and 'fully integrated into the economic life of Asia'. 'As anybody with a sense of history will recognise, the fact that Australians think themselves part of Asia, even to this limited extent, represents a remarkable change in attitudes' (*The Economist* supplement on Australia, 4 April 1992).

Finally, Australia has recognised the importance of the environment and has taken steps to correct past failures and to monitor trends. At the international level Australia has been among the leaders on such matters as the Antarctic Treaty, Climate Control Convention and Biodiversity; and on the domestic front the Threatened Species Bill is now before Parliament, effective action has been taken to deal with beach pollution in Sydney, the bulldozing approach to mining is a thing of the past, much more care is being taken to care for the land and minimise river pollution, a number of watchdog bodies have been set up and efforts are being made to reduce inconsistencies, duplication and long delays in environmental policy decision making at the Federal/State level.

CHAPTER

4

DESIRABLE NATIONAL GOALS FOR THE FUTURE

It is clear we can do better in future. The six tests used to assess our past performance can also serve as a basis for setting *desirable* national goals for the future; and this is the fourth step in the development of a long term strategy for the economy.

The goals we outline below are 'desirable' in that most Australians would accept them as reasonable goals to aspire to. Moreover each one of the goals would, in the opinion of the author, be realistically achievable if sufficient priority were given to it.

However this must not be mistaken for a feasible and viable national vision, since at this stage of the evolution of a national economic strategy the goals have been set in isolation from each other i.e. without regard for possible conflicts between them. This means that while any one of the goals is achievable on its own, the package of goals taken collectively, and therefore the vision as a whole, may not be feasible. In stages 5 and 6 (which are mainly reserved for the final report) conflicts will have to be resolved and the vision as a whole made internally consistent.

The goals may also need to be reviewed in the light of attempts to disaggregate them for operational purposes, and in the light of reactions to this report and the results of a proposed CEDA survey of attitudes.

The goals must therefore be regarded as only provisional and illustrative. They nevertheless serve the useful purpose of offering a framework for assessing trade-offs and the implications of alternative strategic paths.

We start by outlining a set of six primary goals—reflecting the six performance criteria set out earlier—and these are followed by a set of 'intermediate' goals.

(i) Primary goals

Our *first goal* should be to achieve a better growth rate in real incomes per capita. Australians are generally unhappy with what has happened to their living standards over the last twenty years and want to do better (survey results bear this out). Thoughtful Australians are also concerned that our voice and respect in the world may be declining.

A sustainable growth rate in per capita incomes of at least 2% per annum seems a reasonable *minimum* target to set ourselves. It is much better than we achieved in the 1980s and 1970s but below the trend growth of the forty years up to 1973–74 (Maddock 1987).

In fact, because of prospective reductions in unemployment over the next few years (which are discussed below), an 'underlying' (sustainable) increase of at least 2% per annum is consistent with *a growth rate in incomes per head of population of at least 3% per annum over the next five years, followed by at least 2% thereafter*.

Leaving aside once and for all reductions in unemployment, virtually the only sure way to improve per capita incomes on a sustainable basis is through an improvement in productivity per worker. Our per capita goal therefore implies an underlying (trend) rate of increase in output per worker of at least 2% per annum over the next decade, compared with only 1 to 1 and 1/2% over the last couple of decades.

This should be readily achievable and indeed exceeded if employers, employees, unions and governments all give high priority to this goal. The Industry Commission has estimated the long term effect on real GDP of its program of microeconomic reforms (in transport, post and telecommunications, electricity etc.) at 6.5%, although this presumes associated improvements in the flexibility of the labour market and the economy (IC Annual Report 1989–90). In addition the scope for improvements in productivity from changes in work organisation in private industry is recognised to be very great—in individual cases increases of 25 to 30% are achievable through enterprise bargaining or management reforms, according to the Business Council of Australia and the Bureau of Industry Economics.

Not only is a marked acceleration in productivity growth achievable; it is essential if if we want to sustain GDP growth rates of 4% per annum or better without running into frequent balance of payments constraints.

A key element in the Business Council's 'positive vision for Australia' which it presented to the Prime Minister, Mr Keating, in February 1992, was that by the second half of the 1990s 'living standards in Australia are rising at least as fast as our competitors and other advanced economies'; this formulation, while less quantitatively expressed and capable of more than one interpretation, is not necessarily inconsistent with the targets suggested above.

The *second goal* must be greater economic stability than in the past, i.e. we must try to reduce both the amplitude and frequency of economic fluctuations in output and employment.

In quantitative terms a modest target might be, for example, that *growth in real GDP per head should never deviate by more than 50% from the mean growth*. (That is, if the underlying sustainable growth is 2%, the minimum growth must be 1%; and if in the next five years we strive for 3% growth per capita, the minimum increase in any one year must be 1.5%.) This is not too far out of line from the experience of the 1950s and 1960s. It assumes a fairly stable world economic environment, relatively low and stable inflation, and no further blow-out in the net external debt to GDP ratio, so as to avoid periodic 'crises', with a risk of stop-go policy responses. These matters will be considered further in a special CEDA commissioned study.

The *third goal* should be to get as close to sustainable full employment as possible. This goal needs no argument: it is universally seen as desirable because of the potential economic gains, the gains for social cohesion, and above all because it is crucial for the dignity, self-repect and morale of thousands of Australians and their families.

Ideally we should aim to *return to a sustainable unemployment rate of 5% over the next five years or so*. This would require an average growth rate in real GDP of *over* 5% per annum over that period. (This assumes that we attain our 2% productivity growth targe that, with the tendency for participation rates to rise strongly after a recession, the labour supply grows on average by up to 2% per annum.)

Such a growth rate compares with an average annual increase of only 3% in the last decade. It also compares with a growth rate of just over 4%, envisaged in the Government's One Nation scenario for the period 1992–96, which only had an objective of reducing unemployment to 5% *by the end of the decade*.

Clearly, we have set a challenging—some will say impossible—goal for the next few years, but the task becomes easier after the first five years, because the growth rate can then fall back to 3½% per annum without jeopardising the 5% unemployment target.

Some would indeed view the goal of 5% unemployment as too conservative for a national vision. Why not, they ask, go for 2% or 3% by the end of the next decade? After all, we managed that in the 1950s and 1960s and many other countries such as Japan, Austria, Switzerland, Sweden and Singapore have been largely successful in sustaining such rates. The question is a legitimate one, and there is nothing sacred about 5%; but on any plausible assumptions about the speed of labour market and microeconomic reform it is unlikely that a growth rate much in excess of 5% could be sustained in the 1990s without running into balance of payments or inflationary constraints. A 2 to 3% unemployment for the next decade would therefore lack credibility. Nonetheless it deserves consideration for any longer term vision.

The *fourth goal* must be to ensure that the increase in average real incomes over the next two decades is not associated with rising poverty or large and growing inequalities in incomes and wealth. The importance of such a goal was discussed earlier.

This is of course a contentious area. Strictly speaking an economist is not entitled to make interpersonal comparisons of welfare and it is possible to take a 'purist' stance and object to any long term strategy which involved losers as well as winners, even if the winners decisively outnumbered the losers and it was clear that in principle they could more than compensate the losers.

However, this would be a very stultifying constraint. For one thing it assumes that welfare distribution was fair and just in the initial situation, and no one really knows that. More importantly, if one took such a view, economists would have little or nothing to say on policy and there would be virtually no scope for structural reform. This is because few policy changes are 'Pareto improvements' in the sense that they make some better off without making anybody worse off.

We have therefore adopted a less extreme stance here. Bearing in mind concerns noted earlier that marked increases in gross inequality can damage social cohesion and stability, but also keeping in mind the need to reward performance, it is suggested that a reform which increased average real income per head should prima facie be supported even if it involved some redistribution of incomes and wealth, so long as it met three conditions:

- *those below or near the so-called 'poverty line'* (i.e. the critical level that permits a household to buy the basics in food, shelter, clothing, health care and recreation, and generally maintain a dignified existence within a relatively affluent society) *should not be made worse off*, at least in an absolute sense;
- *there should be genuine equality of opportunity in employment, access to health, education etc.* (a condition also included in our quality of life goal below);
- *if a significant section of the community were to be severely disadvantaged by a reform program, an attempt should be made to at least partially compensate the losers*, especially if they were already disadvantaged at the start. This could be done through adjustment programs, through a phasing-in of changes, or more generally through the 'grouping of issues or log rolling' (Abelson 1987).

This is still imprecise. How exactly should the poverty line be defined? What do we mean by genuine equality of opportunity and is that consistent with wide inequalities in wealth and influence? In what circumstances is compensation feasible? However such issues can be deferred until the final report.

Even at the general level adopted here, there will be alternative viewpoints. At one extreme, there are those who would rely almost exclusively on the second (equal opportunity) condition, arguing that as long as there were fair *rules and processes*, the *outcomes* could also be assumed to be fair. Many of these people would want to define the poverty line very narrowly in terms of subsistence (absence of malnutrition or starvation) and, subject to equal opportunity, would want to leave any distributional outcomes above this line entirely to the market place. Nor would they generally favour the principle of compensation. Such views are not supported here as, in the writer's opinion, they leave distributional outcomes too much to the vagaries of the market.

At the other extreme there are those who would argue that the three conditions laid down above do not go far enough. They would see it as necessary and desirable, as part of any national strategy, to explicitly strive for much greater equality of incomes and wealth than at present (as opposed to merely protecting the poor and semi-poor). This view is commendable and many will respond sympathetically to it. However, it is questionable whether it adequately recognises the equity/efficiency trade-off and allows enough room for individual responsibility, self-reliance and self-help, and what many see as a natural right to the fruits of one's work effort. Moreover there are serious problems of measurement in trying to set an income distribution goal that is genuinely fair (few would be prepared to merely accept Gini coefficients and the like).

Finally, a strong and explicit egalitarian view—one which goes well beyond ensuring the conditions are present for genuine equality of opportunity—is unlikely to command wide support in the community. We stressed at the start that a national vision needed to have wide support if it was to have any practical political relevance.

The *fifth goal* must be to *improve the quality of our living environment* in a number of areas: health, quality of air and water, level of noise and traffic congestion, extent of job satisfaction, incidence of crime, availability of social infrastructure etc. As well we need to at least hold on to our gains in areas such as housing standards, choice between work and leisure, access to public recreation facilities etc; and we need to strive to safeguard our basic freedoms and rights and stop further erosion in our economic sovereignty. Such goals are hard to quantify and more work needs to be done to develop a set of quantitative targets.

Sixth, to do the right thing for future Australians, a national long term economic strategy should try to ensure that *the nation's total net wealth (physical, human and natural) increases at least in line with GDP*.

One can go further and argue that as well as ensuring that our successors inherit a stock of *aggregate* physical wealth and human capital, relative to GDP, comparable to what the previous population had, we need to make sure we *fully conserve at least certain crucial parts of our natural wealth*, such as the quality of our air and water and the ecological systems and genetic species that make up diversity; and this goal should be pursued independently of trends in our stock of fixed capital. This can be argued on two grounds: human-made capital offers no real substitute for many forms of natural capital (e.g. ozone layer); and 'the value of natural environments will increase over time' relative to material capital (Harris 1991). On this view, one would have to regard protection of the natural environment as a distinct seventh goal in its own right.

Even Mrs Thatcher warned a few years ago that 'no generation has a freehold on the earth. All we have is a life tenancy—with full repairing lease' (speech to Conservative Party Conference, October 1988).

What the pursuit of inter-generational equity would entail in practice is not clear. At the very least it would mean 'first, using the income gained by the community as a whole from the exploitation of its depletable resources to provide an income for future generations; and second,...maintaining its renewable environmental capital' (Harris 1991).

This proposition will be explored further in the final report; but should the goal of promoting inter-generational equity be adopted in this form, it will need to be disaggregated and defined much more specifically if it is to have any operational significance for policy. For example, if our broad goal is the preservation of certain parts of our natural wealth, we need to know which parts we want to preserve for future generations, and to what extent we want to do so, and then set ourselves particular targets.

Thus, if we want to avoid unpredictable changes in climate in the future, what carbon dioxide and other greenhouse emission levels (mainly energy-related) should we aim for? If it is the atmosphere we want to safeguard because of potential long term implications for human health and for plant life, what levels of production of chlorofluorocarbons (CFCs) and other ozone-destroying chemicals should we tolerate?

If it is our agricultural resources we want to preserve, what should we strive to achieve by way of land rehabilitation? If it is biological diversity and wilderness areas we want to protect, what levels or range of biodiversity would be acceptable and what proportion of our wilderness should be declared national parks? If it is forests we want to protect, what stock of trees should we strive for? If it is the quality of the air, which we want to maintain or improve because of health hazards for the population, what levels of industrial smoke emission, sulphur dioxide concentrations (from power stations etc.) and car energy consumption can we sensibly tolerate? If it is the quality of our water and land resources we want to control, what limits should we set on industrial and agricultural waste production and sewage outflows? And so on.

It should be stressed, however, that the inter-generational equity goal has been set here in isolation from other goals—that is before the trade-off stage, when one has to weigh environmental goals against the economic and social costs. Some of the trade-offs are illustrated in the next chapter but the issue is largely one for the final report.

(ii) Intermediate economic goals

The first three primary goals outlined above for the *first half* of the next decade, taken together, require: average growth of over 3% per annum in real per capita incomes, a gradual reduction to 5% in the unemployment rate, a mean annual real GDP growth of 5% per annum, with a minimum growth rate in any one year of 3% (to ensure a minimum per capita increase of 1.5%), over the period 1991–92 to 1996–97. What intermediate economic goals do we need to strive for to achieve these kinds of results?

First, with an unchanged capital-output ratio, and depending on replacement patterns, we may need to increase our gross investment rate from an average of about 25% of GDP in the 1980s (and much below that in 1991–92) to an average of over 27% of GDP in the projected period.

Second, if we want to stabilise our external liabilities at around 50% of GDP we will need to hold down the current account deficit just below 3% of GDP (EPAC CP 50). Debt stabilisation is included as one of our intermediate goals for three reasons: it is probably a precondition for achieving the desired degree of stability year in year out, as rising foreign debt (and even to some extent foreign equity) levels would make us prone to sudden losses of market confidence, and affect the stability of interest rates, exchange rates and government macroeconomic policy; it is the only sure way to safeguard our economic independence and retain control of our social and economic priorities; and it is an important element in inter-generational equity.

Third, and directly arising out of the first two conditions, we would need to increase our national saving rate from an average of about 20% in the 1980s to an average of over 24% of GDP in the period of the projection.

Fourth, on various possible assumptions about the behaviour of the import coefficient, aggregate export volumes would need to increase by between 8 and 11% per annum, compared with only 5% in the 1980s. (These purely illustrative estimates are based on some preliminary modelling work undertaken for CEDA.)

Fifth, the above conditions would in turn require a sharp improvement in competitiveness, almost certainly in excess of 15% over the five year period projected (again based on early modelling results). Some of that may come from an acceleration in productivity: the Industry Commission has estimated that its program of microeconomic reform had the potential to increase national productivity by at least 6.5% (IC 1990) and various comparative studies of productivity (by the Bureau of Industry Economics, the Business Council of Australia and others) have shown that Australia lags well behind world best practice in many areas of the economy. That said, some of the gains in competitiveness may have to come from a lower level of real wages than might otherwise prevail.

Finally, achievement of the stability goal would almost certainly require that the inflation rate be held down below 3% per annum, or at least not exceed the average rate of our trading partners.

It is unlikely that all these conditions could be met without significant implications for the relative share of wages and profits, the distribution of incomes and wealth, the degree of work place flexibility, workers' rights, and (to the extent that it required strong growth in primary exports, with increased land degradation, chemical residues and exploitation of non-renewable resources) the quality of our natural environment—at least in the short run. Some of the trade-offs may not be acceptable to many Australians.

CHAPTER

5

CHOICES AND PRIORITIES

Having outlined a set of 'desirable' goals, the fifth step in the evolution of a long term strategy is to assess and where possible quantify the trade-offs between the goals, so that we know what are the realistic choices—feasible trade-off opportunities or 'sacrifice ratios'—available to us.

We have already raised the possibility that the six provisional goals we have set ourselves, while highly desirable individually, may be in conflict with each other—i.e. the package may not be internally inconsistent. We may not be able to achieve 2% productivity growth, stable growth, 5% unemployment, an improvement in our quality of life, a more egalitarian income and wealth and income distribution and inter-generational equity *all at the same time.*

Choices may have to be made and priorities set among the various goals for three fundamental reasons: scarce resources; conflicts between different goals; and limited policy instruments relative to policy goals. Let us look briefly at each one in turn.

First, pursuit of desirable national goals generally requires the application of labour, capital, skills and technology and these productive resources are limited over any period. The production possibility curve much used by economists tells us that if we want to produce more of product A we have to divert resources from the production of product B. Exactly the same resource constraint applies to a choice between producing more of product A and say a cleaner environment, to the extent that this requires resources to be applied.

Second, even when resources are available, the goals may conflict because of complex inter-dependencies. The pursuit of some goals or values, such as equity or the environment, often has unavoidable secondary effects which impair our ability to pursue other goals or values, such as higher per capita incomes.

Third, choices have to be made because there are limited policy instruments available to governments for the pursuit of economic goals, so the application of an instrument to one objective may have to be at the expense of another objective. A good example is monetary policy: it can be targetted at short term output/employment or at inflation (stability), but it seldom can efficiently target both.

Every community must therefore choose between conflicting national objectives. Is it possible to pursue policies which will allow us to perform better on all fronts at the same time—or at least do better on one without doing worse on any of the others? In other words, are there positive sum ('Pareto optimising') games we can play in which everyone is better off, including future generations, so that sacrifice ratios do not arise?

The answer is yes but only to a limited degree. There are a few policies, such as those which seek to promote competition, training, work place reform and structural adjustment, which can generally serve as well the aims of efficiency, growth and equity, although even here there may be a few temporary losers. Moreover there some policies which are Pareto-optimising up to a point but not thereafter.

In the discusssion which follows we will point to some of the possible trade-offs as well as some of the complementarities. We will do so under several headings.

(i)
Growth *versus* environment

Environment and growth goals need not be incompatible with each other—indeed, they can mutually reinforce each other.

Up to a point, economic growth is good or at least neutral for the environment: it can provide the increased resources and improvements in technology needed for future environmental improvements, and in that sense it can facilitate the preservation and enhancement of environmental quality. It should also be recognised that lessons have been learned from the mistakes of the past: manufacturing, mining and farming are now conducted in a much more environmentally friendly way than they used to be, with much more attention given to subsequent environmental rehabilitation. The extent to which development conflicts with the environment has been appreciably reduced.

At the other end of the spectrum, there is a point beyond which further indiscriminate economic growth can be bad for both the environment and the economy in the long run. This is when the increase in environmental pollution and reduction in biodiversity have such severe effects on the health and efficiency of the work force, soil quality and fertility, animal productivity, the production and development of pharmaceutical drugs etc., that they damage the long run productive potential of the economy.

Well before such a point is reached, there are many actions a country can take to improve its natural environment which will tend to assist rather than hinder economic growth—e.g. it can adopt a pricing structure for energy and other resources which reflects full social cost; it can pursue active policies of energy conservation and efficiency; it can try to develop environmentally friendly export industries (such as 'clean food', untouched wilderness) which take advantage of the increasing environmental awareness of consumers and tourists; and it can seek to forge a lead role in environmental technology and services to meet the growing demands of relatively polluted areas like East Europe. These can equally serve both economic and environmental goals (note, for example, the success of California and Germany in exploiting these opportunities).

Again, there are many actions which can be taken which will reduce duplication of environmental processes between States and the Commonwealth, and speed up environmental impact statements and policy decisions, and thus help growth without posing any threat to the environment.

Such 'complementarities' are important and they need to be stressed. They demonstrate that within a fairly wide range, more growth is consistent with a better environment and more attention to the environment is consistent with better growth in the long term. In other words, the trade-off curve between growth and the environment is either sloping upwards for a wide range of combinations or the whole curve can with appropriate policies be shifted upwards and to the right.

That said, it must be recognised that the scope for complementarity is rather limited and there remain very real conflicts between growth and the environment which have to be resolved. On the one hand, indiscriminate economic growth can damage the environment in ways which are uncertain and possibly large and irreversible, making it difficult to neutralise future adverse environmental effects out of the returns from future economic growth. There are many types of environmental assets, such as the ozone layer and diversity of species, for which other types of human-made capital cannot substitute. At the very least, such concerns require that an appropriately high value be attached to the benefits of certain forms of environmental investment relative to the benefits from alternative uses of capital or from consumption. This means fully incorporating environmental costs into the appraisal of projects and diverting a sufficient share of the nation's scarce capital to environmental enhancement.

On the other hand, the pursuit of environmental purity can, beyond a point, severely damage economic growth, both in the short and long term. For example, a nation which persistently inhibited export development in the interests of the environment would find that its capacity for economic growth was severely curtailed; and a nation which was so concerned to reduce greenhouse emissions that it set itself much higher environmental standards than the rest of the world may well impose intolerable short term costs on the economy. 'The main certainty about global warming is that its consequences are uncertain and far off, whereas the measures needed to prevent it are immediate and (in some cases) costly' (*The Economist*, 30 May 1992).

In such cases there is a clear trade off between unrestricted short term growth (and the higher material living standards and employment which go with it) and conservation of the natural environment.

Attempts have been made to quantify some of these trade-offs in economic terms. One estimate (Nordhaus 1991) is that about 10% of world greenhouse emissions can be reduced at extremely low cost, but above that level the marginal cost of abatement rises sharply and at some point greatly exceeds the economic cost of greenhouse warming.

Estimates have been made for Australia of the costs of applying an excise tax on the carbon content of primary fuels (coal, oil and gas) to achieve the Commonwealth Government's interim planning target of stabilising emissions of greenhouse gases at 1988 levels by the year 2000 and reducing these emission by 20% by the year 2005. The Industry Commission's study of the effects of Stabilising Carbon Dioxide Emissions (Staff Issues Paper) was followed by a study by London Economics (1992), which concluded that many of our industries like steel and aluminium 'would not survive' if such a tax were imposed unilaterally by Australia or even if it were imposed only by OECD countries; with a global tax the effects would be less severe but still very disadvantageous for Australia.

Similar concerns were expressed by ACIL Australia in its study of The Economic Cost to Australia of Stabilising Carbon Dioxide Emissions in OECD Countries (ACIL May 1992). This envisaged a decline of up to 1.6% in Net National Product and of over 6% in real wages from the required carbon tax. The Australian Bureau of Agricultural and Resource Economics was equally gloomy in its study of the implications for the aluminium industry (ABARE 1992).

Many of these studies, while recognising that carbon tax revenue would permit general tax rates to decline, do not allow for the possibility that the revenue derived from a carbon tax might/can be used to subsidise alternative sources of energy or otherwise compensate the energy-intensive industries affected. They are also very dependent on the particular relationships implicit in their models.

It is clear nevertheless that in this area of greenhouse emissions, as in other areas of the environment (such as preservation of biodiversity and natural wilderness), a point is reached when a higher value can be placed on the environment only at the cost of lower economic growth, at least in the short and medium term. How one would resolve such a perceived 'feasibility trade-off' would depend on how much value one attached to the environment relative to material well being, how much weight one gave to the interests of future generations, how one perceived the ecological risk, how much 'insurance' one felt disposed to take out, given the uncertainties of the scientific evidence on greenhouse emissions, and finally how one assessed the economic cost.

On all these environmental issues there are conflicting views in the community and amongst the scholars (see, for example,

Carruthers 1992, CFF 1991, CIE 1991, ESD Working Groups 1991 and IPEC 1990).

(ii) Growth versus quality of life (economic sovereignty)

As noted earlier, a nation cannot be said to enjoy a high quality of life if it does not have complete freedom to choose its own social and economic priorities, without pressure or interference from foreign markets, multinationals companies or international bodies. Yet the uninhibited pursuit of growth by a capital importing country like Australia (in the same way as a country tied to a currency bloc) may of necessity require some loss of national economic independence. For example, EPAC's 'slow external adjustment path' would involve an increase in foreign ownership of Australia's private corporate sector from the present 35% of issued equity to perhaps 45% (EPAC CP 50 1992). If the community was not prepared to increase its saving rate (and thereby move to a faster adjustment path) it would have to choose between accepting an increase in foreign ownership or slowing down economic growth.

Those who advocate restrictions on foreign capital inflow are in effect advocating slower economic growth (in the absence of a higher saving rate). If, for example, restrictions were imposed on foreign ownership and control in order to preserve a greater degree of economic independence we would not only be lowering our sustainable rate of investment but also denying ourselves some of the technological, productivity and employment benefits of foreign direct investment, and hence achievement of another national goal—higher real per capita incomes. Similarly if we were to restrict or discourage foreign borrowing in order to protect our long run economic sovereignty, we would gain some independence but at the cost of a decline in our growth potential.

There is, as noted earlier, some basis for concern about our growing external indebtedness and the difficulty Australia has had in reconciling strong economic growth with sustainable current account deficits; but policies to restrain capital inflow would merely address symptoms rather than causes. The underlying causes—a deficiency in saving, a low return on investment and a gap in competitiveness—

were discussed in an earlier section. They would need to be addressed. Of course even the route of higher saving and productivity would not be painless and would involve different kinds of trade-offs in the short run.

(iii) Growth versus equity

As with the environment/growth interaction, there is a good deal of complementarity between equity and growth.

There is a point beyond which egalitarian policies can, if pushed further, seriously disturb the balance between effort, skill or intelligence on the one hand and reward on the other. At that point they can markedly damage the growth potential of the economy. It can be argued that when this point is reached, attempts to achieve greater 'equality' would not only be bad for growth but also for 'equity'—in two senses: first, such a degree of equality could be viewed as inherently unfair (in that it fails to adequately reward effort); and secondly, it could prove counter-productive in the long run for the poor, in so far as it led to a reduction in both the wherewithal and the will to pay for a generous welfare system. In such cases there is no real conflict between equity and growth.

Equally, there is a point beyond which increasing income and wealth disparities must be as harmful for growth as for equity: you cannot maintain for long an efficient, stable economy with wide class differences, depressed wages, poor working conditions and extreme job insecurity (EPAC CP 35 1988).

Between these two points, however, there is a wide range within which there is scope for the community to trade off equity against efficiency gains.

Economists have long debated the nature of this trade-off. Some have argued that a 'generous' welfare system (especially provisions for the elderly) reduces the incentive to save (e.g. White 1991, Clarnette 1988, Keynes 19, pp. 18–22); that high unemployment benefits discourage employment (Clarnette 1988, Lehmann in *The Australian*, 18 March 1992, and Minford 1988); that tightly means-tested welfare benefits cause 'poverty traps' (Brownlee 1985; Saunders and Whiteford, Australian Tax Forum); and that high marginal tax rates, which may be required to finance redistributive policies, impact adversely on work, saving, investment and innovation (Aaron 1984, Lindbeck 1986, Browning 1987). A strongly argued view on these issues can be found in the submission by the Institute of Public Affairs to the 1988 Inquiry by the Catholic Bishops' Committee of Justice (Clarnette 1988).

The nature of these relationships is rather conjectural and the evidence somewhat inconclusive (EPAC CP 35 1988, and Stilwell 1992). For example, it can be argued that the effects of changes in income distribution on saving rates are fairly small, and that other influences (such as income levels, inflation, interest rates, net wealth and demographic changes) are more important for long term saving rates (EPAC CP 36 1988, and papers in P. Stemp (ed.) 1991).

Judgments are necessarily involved on such issues, and these will often be influenced by ideology. Thus conservative governments will tend to attach excessive importance to the potential economic benefits of a less progressive tax system. It has been argued, for example, that the sharp increase in inequality in the UK in the Thatcher years 'could have been mitigated by different tax and benefits policies without seriously jeopardising the productivity improvements, which probably did not depend on personal tax cuts' (Crafts 1991).

The point to note here is that if growth policies are well constructed they can often achieve a large part of their objective without adverse social effects. The trade-off will still remain but the 'sacrifice ratio' can be greatly reduced. Similarly, social policies can be designed in such a way as to minimise adverse effects on growth. This is true, for example, of training and retraining programs for the unemployed (like Newstart).

That said, there remains a wide range of tax and welfare policy options where the community perceives a choice between more equity, in the form of lesser income and wealth inequality, and more economic growth.

Conflicts between efficiency and equity do not only arise in the areas of welfare and taxation policy. Similar conflicts are evident, for example, in industry policy. It is generally accepted that many of the microeconomic reforms advocated by the Industry Commission, and projected changes to manufacturing industry assistance, would have significant implications for regional, industrial patterns of employment and income distribution (EPAC CP 46, Industry Commission Information Paper No. 7 1991). These effects may be partly transitional (where redeployment of workers is possible over a reasonable period of time) and partly sustained (where the displaced workers, because of age, low learning capacity etc. join the long term unemployed). Such effects can be cushioned in various ways e.g. by phasing in proposed changes, but this might involve delaying some of the efficiency benefits.

There are thus circumstances in which a nation has to make choices between equity and growth. If it were to decide that equity merited higher priority, it may choose:

- to generously help the poor notwithstanding possible economic disincentive effects, e.g. on saving;
- to shun relatively 'efficient' taxes (such as a lump sum or poll tax) simply because they were inequitable;
- to protect vulnerable workers and consumers from exploitation even to the point where it may have adverse effects on business investment, innovation and competitiveness;
- to opt for a more gradual pace of microeconomic and structural reform e.g. in regard to tariff reductions or the application of user pays principles in the public sector;
- to cushion the effects on the 'casualties of change' by providing generous adjustment assistance to people affected by government-induced technological and structural change, despite the implications for tax levels and incentives.

On the other hand, a nation may prefer in all these instances to give higher priority to economic growth and accept the short to medium term social costs.

(iv)
Equity versus equity

Many policy decisions involve not only conflicts between equity and efficiency but also between alternative social goals. One example is the perceived trade-off between improving average real wages on the one hand and reducing long term unemployment on the other.

Many economists believe that it is possible to reduce the incidence and duration of unemployment among the more vulnerable sections of the labour force—the young, older workers, unskilled—by lowering minimum wage and conditions, and that their employment gains would be only partially at the expense of other workers. (It is not of course the only way to assist disadvantaged workers: retraining and other labour market programs, including wage subsidies, can also assist in this regard.) It is also often argued more generally that the employment potential of the economy would be greater if workers in jobs were more willing to forego increases in real wages and various benefits of employment, and if employers had greater freedom to vary working time arrangements, and hire and fire.

These claims are still the subject of debate (see articles and correspondence in *Australian Financial Times*, June 1991). They are likely to have most validity where a country acts unilaterally to reduce wages and achieves an improvement in its competitive position vis-à-vis the rest of the world. If the claims are accepted, they point to a path of lower pay as a partial solution to lower unemployment.

This path, which many see as (in part) the one chosen by New Zealand, can mean—at least in the short run—a fall in living standards of many workers. To the extent that wage cuts are reflected in lower domestic prices for consumers, the standard of living of workers as a whole would not be affected. Again, if the changes are associated with strong productivity gains, there need be no cost to the workers (and indeed they can share in the gains). However, many of the cost-cutting and increased flexibility proposals of employers simply involve the withdrawal of existing or potential benefits of employment and imply—initially at least—a redistribution of incomes from wage earners to profit earners and to foreign consumers. Even in those cases the workers in question may be better off in the long run if the cost reductions make the economy more competitive, but for quite a lengthy period they are likely to be clearly worse off. The fear is that, at the extreme, this could 'create an under-class of employed people on very low wages—the working poor' (Minister for Industrial Relations, Senator Cook, quoted recently in *The Australian*).

The choice is between assisting one group of socially disadvantaged workers—the unemployed—or maintaining the living standards of people in jobs, some of whom are not at all well off and are heavily committed.

Some will say this is a false analogy as the standard of living of workers can be protected through the tax and transfer system, which is in any case a more efficient instrument of social policy than the wage system. However, given the strong and growing resistance to taxes and the incentive problems noted earlier, this alternative course is not as readily available as is often implied.

(v)
Growth, low unemployment versus stability

While economists generally agree that in the long run there is no trade-off between unemployment and inflation, there is clear evidence that governments cannot, through the application of monetary policy, permanently reduce the rate of inflation (say to zero) without a temporary but costly loss of output and employment. In Australia, estimates by EPAC suggest that the cumulative transitional output costs of reducing inflation by 1% (using monetary policy) can be as high as 2.5% for output and 3% for unemployment (Murphy, EPAC Background Paper No.11, p. 8, 12), but higher estimates have also been produced (Carmichael & Nguyen).

Such short run costs are to be found in most countries. In the USA the consensus estimate is that 6% of a year's output must be sacrificed to reduce inflation permanantly by 1% (Robert Gordon in *The Economist*, 14 March 1992); the costs appear to be somewhat lower in Japan and higher in the UK (V. Argy, chapters 6 and 22). The key factors determining the so-called 'sacrifice ratio' are the degree of wage/price flexibility and the credibility of monetary policy.

Governments therefore have a choice: in the absence of structural change, they can opt to pursue monetary policies which will permit lower unemployment in the short run but with the risk of higher inflation and eventually greater instability in the longer term; or they can tolerate higher unemployment in the short run in the hope that it will be able to maintain a steadier and perhaps more dynamic growth path in the longer term.

Similar choices between long term growth and short term stability occur in other policy areas. For example, a government can choose to give overriding priority to reducing the current account deficit because of the perceived risks for the long term stability and growth potential of the economy, or it can prefer to go for short term growth and deal with problems such as loss of financial market confidence and increased vulnerability to future shocks if and when they arise.

The Australian Government generally leaned towards the first position (i.e giving relatively high priority to the current account deficit) throughout the 1980s—hence the drastic action to slow growth in both 1985–86 and 1988–89; but a subtle change in relative priorities may be occurring. The Prime Minister is reported as saying that it was time to 'shift away from the safe course of accepting lower rates of growth' and 'take a macroeconomic risk on inflation and the current account deficit to get faster growth' (*Australian Financial Review*, 29 January 1992).

Similar conflicts between growth and stability arise when governments have to choose between the efficiency benefits of free trade and open and vigorous domestic competition on the one hand, or the greater certainty, security and stability offered by sheltered markets on the other. If a government were to opt for protection and diversification of its industry base in order to promote greater economic stability and higher employment, it would probably be at the cost of some productivity growth—a cost which many are apparently prepared to accept ('I would think we could accept a degree of inefficiency in order to retain a diversified economy': Prof. Colin White, reported in *The Australian*, April 1992).

It should be added that some studies challenge the view that interventionist industry policies, including targetted investment incentives, necessarily reduce productivity growth (see scenarios prepared for Vision 10 issued by the Manufacturing Council of Victoria 1992), but Industry Commission simulations point clearly in that direction. (See also Jonson 1992.)

Again, a Government may decide that the integrity of banks, other major financial institutions and capital markets is so important for economic stability and equity, that it is prepared to regulate to protect small investors even to a point where the effects on economic growth become negative, e.g. because of high compliance costs and adverse implications for flexibility, innovation, the supply of risk capital and the risk spectrum available to investors.

In brief, while some policy reforms can give us the best of all worlds, there are likely to be many areas where pursuit of one goal or set of goals will be detrimental to the achievement of other goals. To address these trade-offs it is important to know the nature of the 'sacrifice ratio' or feasible trade-offs. The CEDA project will try to make a contribution in this area but we do not under-estimate the complexities.

Setting priorities

Assessing the feasible trade-offs is not enough, however. Understanding the nature of the conflict between the goals—the set of alternatives available to society—is one thing; but how does one determine what relative value or weight to attach to these goals, so as to decide on national priorities? An important step in any long term economic strategy must be to compare feasible trade-off opportunities with preferred trade-offs, and decide on the appropriate direction to proceed to achieve an appropriate optimal equilibrium position.

A key requirement here is information on the community's preferences, or its 'social indifference curve' as it is sometimes called: how much growth would it be prepared to actually give up to, say, improve the natural environment or increase equality? Conversely, how much additional inequality, air and water pollution etc. would the community be willing to tolerate in pursuit of economic growth?

Are such questions capable of a sensible answer? Whose preferences are we trying to assess? Those of the majority? How does one add up the preferences of different individuals in society? Is it reasonable to assume that in our political system the Government's preferences ultimately reflect those of the majority?

The CEDA project will try to throw light on these questions. We have conducted an opinion survey and reviewed the findings of other surveys. These will help indicate people's preferences and priorities, but here too the task is daunting in its complexity.

CHAPTER

6

GOVERNMENT ROLE AND ALTERNATIVE STRATEGIES

Once we have assessed the trade-offs and set priorities, we can design an internally consistent, viable national vision (or set of alternative visions). That done, the next step in the development of a long term national economic strategy is to decide on the role which governments should play in furthering the vision's goals. This is where the heart of the debate lies in Australia.

The question of the government's role involves philosophical and socio-political issues which do not lend themselves to scientific verification. Cross country studies show no clear relationship between size of government and long term economic performance and in any case Australia does not have a particularly large public sector (EPAC CP 49). The issues must largely be addressed in theoretical terms.

(i)
Two views on government interventionism

Market systems can be classified along a continuous spectrum depicting different degrees of intervention. In the Australian context we can exclude the extremes of laissez faire and central planning but the realistic options are still wide enough to leave a significant spectrum of choice.

At one end of the spectrum we have what we will call the libertarian school. This believes that market prices, firms and individuals, operating in a competitive environment, should be the main driving force of change. Apart from clear-cut cases of market failure, where there might be grounds for public intervention, the Government should merely set the legal and regulatory framework in which fair and efficient markets can operate and enforce the laws impartially. (This view is evident, for example, in Jonson 1992.)

At the other end we have what we will call the statist or 'dirigiste' school which believes in a vibrant, active govern-ment sector—one which not only heavily regulates markets but often by-passes them, and pursues active interventionist policies.

To some extent the disagreement between the two schools reflects a different set of relative values and priorities. Thus, those who favour a relatively insular, statist economic strategy tend also to attach great weight to such values as national sovereignty, employment security and stability, and fair distributional outcomes. The other school tends to put more stress on economic efficiency and development, low inflation, and on such values as individual freedom of choice, individual responsibility, self-help, self-reliance (less dependence on government) and equality of opportunity.

As a result of these philosophical differences, the two schools might have different objectives e.g. in regard to poverty, distributive justice and worker protection.

However the disagreement is less often about national goals and values and more often about:

- the *cost-effectiveness* of government intervention in achieving given aims, and in particular about whether governments can out-perform the markets; and
- where intervention is desirable, the most appropriate policy instruments or *methods of intervention* to use to correct for market failure.

(ii)
Scope and cost effectiveness of intervention

On the question of the extent to which government intervention is cost effective, the issue hinges on what governments are and are not good at.

Both schools agree that the market is far from perfect and that governments have a clear responsibility not only to provide an appropriate macroeconomic environment, but also to correct where it can for market imperfections (e.g. by requiring minimum information disclosure and prohibiting certain types of anti-competitive behaviour) and ensure an adequate supply of 'public goods'. [Public goods, very broadly defined, are socially desirable goods and services which the community needs to have but which it is not sensible to leave solely to the market, either because it is not possible to exclude certain users, or because the goods cannot be viably produced by more than one or two producers, or because the social net benefits tend to exceed private net benefits (externalities) so the market will tend to chronically under-supply. Examples are parks and gardens, the police, electricity reticulation, areas of education and health, and protection of the environment.]

Beyond that, however, there is a wide area of disagreement on the appropriate role of governments. This is especially evident on the question of industry policy and the role it should play in improving competitiveness and economic growth.

The statist school has faith in the ability of governments to intervene effectively to correct for what they see as frequent failure of markets to allocate resources in an optimum way—failures which they believe occur because markets are ill-informed or unduly myopic or risk averse or too swayed by speculative influences.

The libertarian school accepts that such market failures can and do occur, but it believes that government intervention would tend, more often than not, to produce an even worse outcome than the market. Governments, they say, are generally less able to pick future successful industries or sectors than the market; as well they tend to become captives of rent-seeking lobby groups or firms and find it hard to extricate themselves once an error of judgment is recognised. Moreover, as a result of their intervention, there has to be a rise in taxes or wages or interest rates or the exchange rate, and this tends to crowd out some otherwise viable marginal industries. Finally, it is argued, governments are generally stretched to the limit and if they become involved in detailed industry planning they may be forced to neglect some of their core tasks.

(iii) Methods of intervention

As noted earlier, the two schools disagree not only on the extent to which government intervention is effective in achieving its intended ends, but also on the appropriate methods of intervention.

Governments can intervene through direct spending and production decisions, through the tax structure, through new regulation (direct government controls over prices, entry conditions, quality of service etc.), or by removing regulatory or monopolistic impediments to the efficient functioning of markets.

The mix of instruments favoured by the libertarians differs markedly from that favoured by the statists. This can be illustrated first with respect to industry development and then with respect to social and other issues.

Industry development

If it was considered that the economy was lacking in competitiveness, the libertarian school would seek to fix the problem by making markets function better e.g. through removal of barriers to domestic competition, a better flow of information, tax reform to deal with any cost handicaps in trade-exposed sectors, and deregulation of the labour market to enhance the flexibility and efficiency of enterprises. To improve public sector efficiency it would seek to remove price distortions and featherbedding, whether through privatisation or corporatisation of public enterprises, or through introducing greater competition, either directly or via competitive tendering. It would also look to smaller government and lower taxes, together with an efficient pricing system, to provide a better incentive climate.

Any industry assistance would be designed to impact equally across the economy and to preserve a level playing field.

The statist school would support active government intervention in financial market flows and use of the tax structure to influence private resource allocation decisions and guide the development of the economy. It would lean towards a centralised wage system, a prices and incomes policy and a corporatist approach to contain cost pressures. Within the limits of fiscal prudence, it would seek to build up the nation's productive public infrastructure. And so on.

Other policy areas

Similar disagreements between the libertarian and statist schools can be seen in other areas of policy, with the disagreement mainly centred around what is the most effective *method* of intervention. Thus:

- in pursuit of *social goals*, libertarians would first look for ways of substituting private welfare (welfare organisations, family and social networks) for public welfare, where the former can deliver the service as or more efficiently. Where public instruments of income support are used, they would be inclined to rely overwhelmingly on transfers to individuals through the tax/welfare system (e.g. a negative income tax and targetted education or health vouchers)—in preference to other methods of redistribution such as (a) the direct provision of services or (b) indirect methods, such as wage and financial regulation, or the pricing structure of government business enterprises, or the universal provision of health and education programs, that are more remote from the main purpose in hand and interfere more with the efficient functioning of markets and the exercise of free choice. On the other hand, the statists would be happy to use the full gamut of available government instruments—financial and wage regulation, government business enterprise pricing policies etc. to further their social goals;
- in the case of *environment* protection, libertarians would try to work through rather than by-pass the market e.g. they would make use of taxes, subsidies, tradeable permits and the like to ensure that prices reflected the full social, and not just the private, cost of energy burning or car-driving or waste-dumping. On the other hand, statists would be at least as inclined to use direct regulation;
- in striving for *macro-economic stability*, libertarians would lean towards market-based instruments and would set their monetary and fiscal stance in a medium term framework. They would also attach high importance to the control of inflation (mainly because

of its capacity to distort market signals and impede competitiveness) even at the risk of higher short term unemployment, and would give the Reserve Bank a single inflation target and more independence from Government. On the other hand, statists would be more concerned about short term unemployment than inflation, and more inclined towards counter-cyclical demand management ('fine tuning'); they would use monetary policy for a mix of economic objectives and would not be averse to employing some direct controls at times;

- in addressing *structural unemployment*, libertarians would rely heavily on real wage flexibility and reform of the incentive system, whereas the statists would rely relatively more on labour market and other active employment programs.

(iv) More interventionism or less?

On all these matters of disagreement the central issue is the role and effectiveness of government intervention. One school of thought is in fact proposing quite different long term economic strategies from the other.

We do not have to embrace in toto one or the other ideology. A long term economic strategy seeks to address a wide range of problems. Some lend themselves better to libertarian solutions while other problems are better addressed by using statist-type solutions. This is a topic for the final report but a few illustrations are in order here.

Take the federal system. It can be argued that it needs some radical reform of the kind espoused by the libertarians, and that the centralist leanings of the statist school are a hindrance to rationalisation and harmonisation.

It is also now widely agreed that the industrial relations system needs to be drastically reformed, but this is already happening and most statists have abandoned any idea of returning to a highly regulated wage structure. The only relevant question is how fast and how far we move towards a decentralised industrial relations system.

When the question is put in this form, it is at least arguable that the libertarian approach to industrial relations is both right and wrong. It is right in wanting to see a faster pace of change in union structures: until unions are reorganised into enterprise-based bargaining units, with their first obligation being to the prosperity and success of the enterprise, the full potential for productivity gains in the work place will not be realised. On the other hand, some libertarians want to abandon altogether any role for trade unions and the Industrial Relations Commission, and are prepared to allow an erosion in minimum standards for wages and conditions; although in theory defensible (the wage system is an inappropriate instrument of income redistribution), such an approach may be too confrontationist and socially divisive, having regard to the uncertain size of the 'additional' efficiency gains to be had (i.e. additional to what is achievable through enterprise bargaining under the present and evolving industrial relations rules) and the risks for macro wage stability. (This issue is the subject of further study by CEDA.)

The UK experience in the 1980s is interesting. It is true that the Thatcher trade union reforms weakened the bargaining power of workers over such issues as manning levels and technological change; and this, in conjunction with a tougher and more credible monetary stance (with its implicit threat of unemployment), may have contributed to the much improved productivity performance of the UK economy in the 1980s.

However, the other Thatcher supply side reforms, in particular the increase in domestic product market competition, were probably more important in achieving the undoubtedly impressive productivity results; and there were social costs in the form of a sharp increase in income inequalities and (for a period at least) an appreciable increase in unemployment. Moreover, the more decentralised system of wage bargaining did nothing at all to stop the tendency for wages to rise faster, relative to productivity, in the UK than in its European partners (EPAC Council Paper 47, p. 38). However, the more recent New Zealand reforms seem to have produced somewhat different outcomes, and CEDA will be studying closely that experience in further work proposed on this project.

We also pointed earlier to the possibility that a perverted incentive structure may have inhibited our productivity performance. This can often be traced back to a distorted tax system, tariffs, irrational pricing policies or bad regulation. The libertarians are on the right track in wanting to review critically all these areas.

On industry policy the Government has an important reformist role, but, in the view of the writer, this should be in the direction suggested by the libertarian school—i.e. towards a true level playing field. There is no salvation in either a return to general protectionism or in a selective sectoral approach to industry support. In general, governments neither have superior information to the market nor effective tools at their disposal to address the problem, and they tend to be distracted by rent-seekers.

However, the view of libertarians on the role of government in correcting for market failure may perhaps be too limited. Governments should be actively seeking to help markets work better by ensuring they are well-informed. They should require adequate disclosure to consumers and investors even if it involves some increase in business costs and reduction in flexibility. Equally, governments have a role to facilitate the flow of information to smaller businesses on technological developments and export markets, and should be prepared to assist in providing a mechanism for cooperative research and development, and to intervene actively in promoting training.

A case can even be made, given Australia's acute balance of payments and debt problems, for policies which tilt the playing field in favour of traded goods as a whole (as opposed to supporting particular industries or activities). The Government has already moved a little in that direction in its One Nation Package of February 1992.

There is also an argument for making greater use of structural adjustment assistance programs as a means of spreading the costs of industrial reform and widening support for such reform.

As for failures of macroeconomic policy, the lesson drawn by the libertarian school—that fine tuning is counter-productive and governments should abandon such attempts and rely solely on automatic stabilisers—is too extreme. While reliance on fine tuning certainly needs to be reduced, there is still a role for discretionary fiscal policy, and it would be sensible to 'put more resources into attempts to improve forecasting' (Pitchford 1992), as well as seeking ways of making fiscal policy more automatically sensitive to changes in demand (*The Economist*, March 1992).

Designing a program of reform

The eighth step in designing a long term economic strategy is to draw up an integrated program of specific reforms.

As indicated at the start, this paper will not attempt to outline such a program—a task reserved for the final report. However, some of the observations above on the role of government indicate at least the general direction of the writer's thinking on some of the key elements of a reform program.

CHAPTER

7

IMPLEMENTATION PROBLEMS

Once the broad strategy is determined, and a policy reform package put together, the final step in the development of a long term economic strategy is to devise an effective plan of implementation. Here, there are three major constraints to overcome—attitudinal, institutional and technical.

(i) Attitudinal barriers

The attitudinal constraint reflects public apathy, ignorance and myopia. To overcome this constraint, governments have to do more than simply respond to community preferences and aspirations. They must educate, mobilise and galvanise public opinion. In particular they must explain the costs and benefits of alternative paths, and the reasons why some options are not feasible or desirable; and, once they have made up their mind on which way they want the nation to go, they must try to build a majority coalition of winners in the community, mobilise this coalition to campaign for change, and neutralise at least some of their opponents, where necessary through compensation (Marsh 1990, p. 184).

Consultation and consensus-building are an important means of smoothing the process of implementation, especially in a country like Australia where there is nothing approaching a national consensus on even key issues such as growth, equity and the environment. While consultative processes can slow down the reform process at times, they should, if done well, contribute to a more effective, less wasteful and perhaps fuller implementation of the desired reform program.

First, as a result of the consultation process, the Government is better informed about community concerns and objections and can take these into account before implementation; as a result the quality of policy decisions improves.

Second, it leads to a better understanding among interest groups in the community of the nation's problems and challenges, of the constraints on governments, of the incompatibility of their demands and expectations with those of other important groups (a learning experience most notably available from broadly based multi-interest consultative forums like EPAC), and of the reasons for proposed reforms. As a result there is wider acceptance of the reforms when they are implemented, and therefore less social and industrial tension associated with the reform process.

Third, the consensus approach helps to weaken the effects of sectionalism (which we identified earlier as a factor in our poor economic performance). 'The adoption of policies characterised by corporatist overtones served to reinforce the role and status of (these) more encompassing groups, contributing to an environment in which the pressure exerted by narrow sectional groups was more effectively countervailed' (Keating & Dixon 1989, pp. 67–8).

A further rationale of the corporatist approach is that sectional groups can have regard for the wider national interest without fear that other groups will benefit at their expense.

Finally, and largely as consequence of the points already made, corporatism leads to changes in the influence of 'insiders' (e.g trade union members) relative to 'outsiders' (such as the unemployed) in wage bargaining and other market decisions. It thus reduces the short term costs of implementing certain policy reforms such as wage restraint or structural change (B. Chapman 1991, Flateau et al. in Johnson 1991).

It can be argued that Australia has never had a fully fledged 'corporatist' approach in place—it merely had a Government-Union accord—and that it was not therefore able to derive the benefits that other corporatist countries were able to derive (Castles 1992), and this is undoubtedly true.

Nonetheless the Government developed a consistent and constructive process of consultation with broad-based peak bodies like the ACTU, the BCA, ACOSS, the Council of Professions etc., whose interests were less at variance with national economic priorities than those of their more narrowly based affiliates; through this process the relative strength and influence of the narrower groups was reduced.

This in turn provided a more favourable climate for reform—clearly evident, for example, in the evolution of the debate on industry protection (Keating & Dixon 1989, p. 68). It also contributed to lower aggregate wage outcomes and lower industrial disputation (Chapman 1991), although there may well have been costs in terms of slower microeconomic and public sector reform in some areas, and a less flexible fiscal policy (Moore 1990).

(ii) System of governance

Whatever the care taken with consultation and consensus-building and whatever the level of leadership shown by governments, the task of implementation can be assisted or impeded by the institutional framework—what has been called the system of governance.

Governability—the extent to which the responsible policy-makers of a country are able to make and carry out policy on behalf of their citizens—is enhanced if first, the nation is united and cohesive and has a real sense of nationhood, and second, there is in place a political and electoral system which facilitates or at least does not hinder long term policy making, i.e. there is a strong executive which can get things done, but within a vibrant democracy.

Australia goes a certain way towards meeting the first requirement, although it still lacks a full sense of nationhood. It may however be handicapped in regard to the second requirement. While it can be argued that the system of preferential voting in single-member constituencies (for the House of Representatives), coupled with our disciplined two-party system, has generally produced stable and responsible government at the federal level, effective government has been impeded by our federal structure, with its three layers of government and often overlapping and conflicting jurisdictions; by our three to four-year parliamentary terms and frequency of elections; and by the apathy and myopia of voters, and their cynical and suspicious attitude towards politicians.

Of course, a strong executive arm of government is only attainable within limits in a democracy. While some might be prepared to subordinate democracy to the needs of the economy, the overwhelming majority of Australians would reject such views with contempt (see critique of these views by P.P. McGuinness in *The Australian*, 20 February 1992). In any case the more recent literature does not support the proposition that a degree of autocracy is conducive to stronger economic performance (Lane & Ersson 1990, pp. 140–4).

That said, there is room for significant reform of the system of governance in Australia without in any way diluting the strength of our democratic institutions. These issues will be addressed in another CEDA project.

(iii) Technical policy constraints

Apart from institutional and attitudinal constraints on policy implementation, there are also technical constraints on the ability of governments to control the economy. For one thing, the tools and data available to governments and their economic advisers are not sufficiently refined to enable them to forecast and respond quickly to changes in the economic environment, or to predict accurately and confidently the impact of various policy and institutional reforms on saving, investment, exports, productivity and so on.

These technical constraints on effective policy implementation are compounded by the nature of the market environment which governments face: many key decisions bearing on productivity and competitiveness are made by individuals and enterprises rather than governments; our economy is particularly prone to frequent and unexpected economic fluctuations because of our dependence on commodity prices; and in an interdependent, highly integrated world, governments here, like everywhere, are heavily constrained by developments in financial and foreign exchange markets.

CHAPTER

8

CONCLUDING COMMENTS

This paper sought to provide a brief, panoramic view of the issues which need to be addressed in designing a long term national economic strategy. Many of the views expressed are exploratory rather than final and there are few if any policy prescriptions in the paper.

Nevertheless some important conclusions can be drawn from the evidence and arguments presented in this paper.

First, the public debate about the economy needs to be re-oriented away from short term developments towards an integrated set of long term national goals; and there is a corresponding need to inject a longer term strategic perspective into day to day policy decisions. There are encouraging signs that the political and policy debate is now moving in that direction.

Second, any long term economic strategy must recognise the multi-dimensional character of people's hopes and aspirations and the complexity of values in the community. It cannot be too narrowly centred on monetary goals.

Third, whichever way we choose to assess our economic performance—in narrow monetary terms or in terms of wider criteria which embrace social, quality of life and environmental values—we have not been high achievers over the last twenty years. We must strive to do better in future.

Fourth, we must recognise that we have, and always will have, a basically private enterprise economy and that the dynamism of such an economy must critically depend on the incentive climate, i.e. relative prices and rewards. It is therefore vital to reassess all government interventions to ensure they are not having perverse effects on decisions to save, invest, innovate and export. At the same time markets often do fail and ideological opposition to all forms of government intervention in the economy is not a logically sustainable proposition.

Fifth, a national economic strategy must face up squarely to the inevitability of conflict among the various national goals, and not run away from the need to make hard choices and set priorities. This means looking at goals collectively rather than individually, with a view to developing an internally consistent and integrated national vision. It means a willingness to question even long-established institutions and beliefs, and it is heartening to see that not only protection but even sacred cows like immigration, housing and the industrial relations and federal systems are currently being subjected to vigorous debate and are accepted as legitimate targets of structural reform.

Finally, although this paper is on the whole very critical of our economic performance over the last two decades, there is reason to look to the future with some confidence. As we stressed in the paper, the 1980s have seen a radical transformation in attitudes and important reforms in the work place and in the incentive climate. In that sense the past decade has sown the seeds for a future economic renaissance.

It is hoped that this paper will generate public debate and discussion, and that this will help CEDA to design a long term national vision and strategy which best meets the long term aspirations of Australians.

GRAPHS AND TABLES

Figure 1

REAL GDP

PERCENTAGE DEVIATIONS FROM TREND

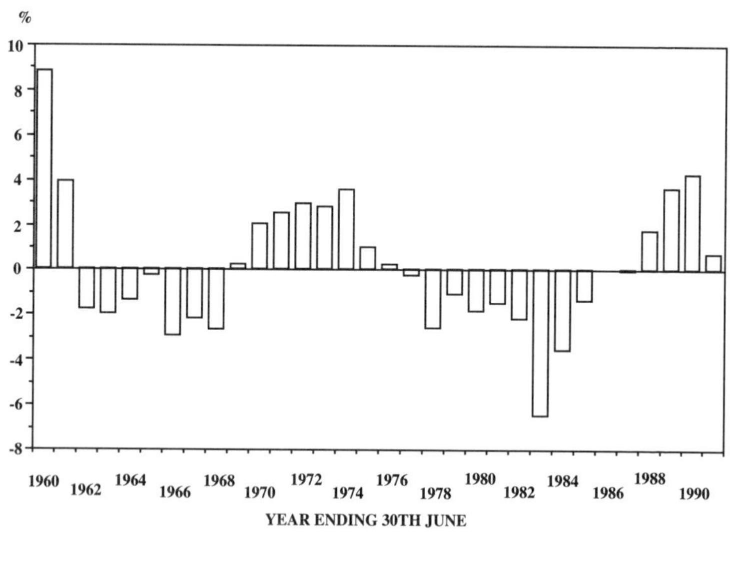

Source: Australian National Accounts: National Income and Expenditure, 1990-91. ABS Cat. No. 5204.0.
Table 77, Expenditure on Gross Domestic Product at Average 1984-85 Prices.
Australian National Accounts: National Income and Expenditure, March Q. 1992. ABS Cat. No. 5206.0.
Table 50, Gross Domestic Product at Average 1984-85 Prices.

Figure 2

ANNUAL INFLATION, 1961-1991

AUSTRALIA AND OECD

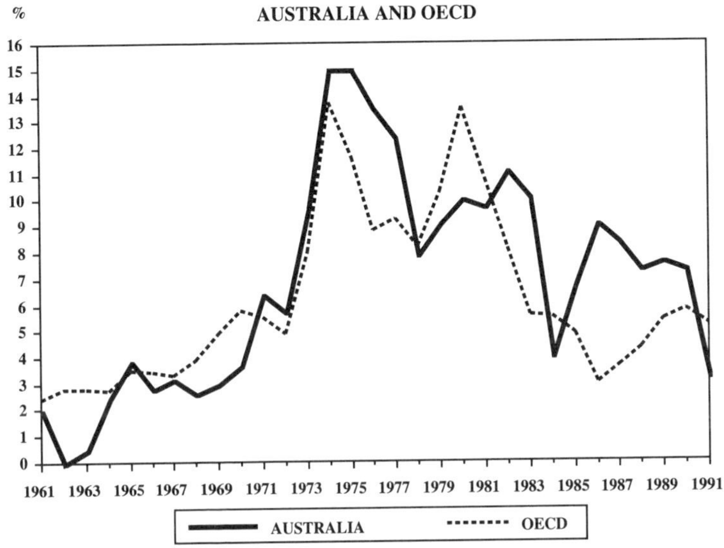

Source: Consumer Price Index, March Q. 1992. ABS Cat. No. 6401.0. Table 1. Consumer Price Index: All Groups Index Numbers
Australian Economic Statistics: 1949-50 to 1989-90, by RA Foster and SE Stewart. Reserve Bank of Australia. Occasional Paper No. 8, Feb. 1991. Table 6.23 Consumer Prices. p. 288.
OECD Main Economic Indicators database. Reuters Numerical Services.

Figure 3

EXTERNAL LIABILITIES AS A % OF GDP

AUSTRALIA, 1969 TO 1991

Year end June 30

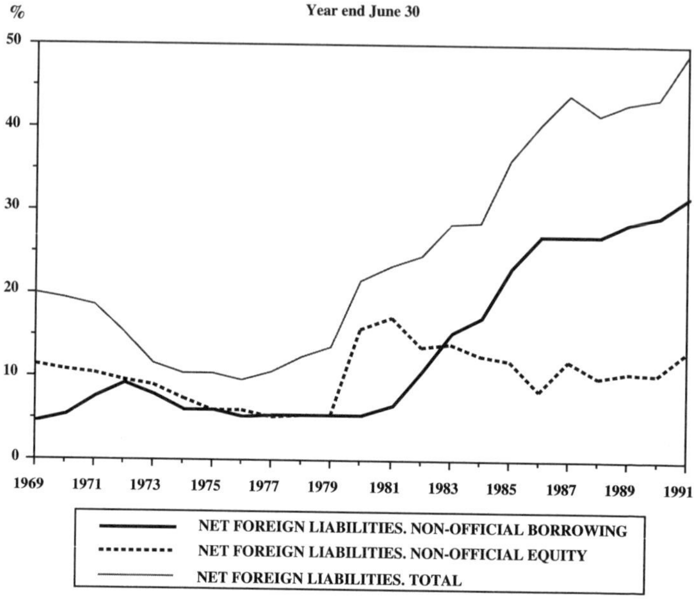

Source: International Investment Position Australia, March Q., 1992. ABS Cat. No. 5306.0. Table 6. Level sof Investment at end of Period.
Australian Economic Statistics: 1949-50 to 1989-90, by RA Foster and SE Stewart.. Reserve Bank of Australia. Occasional Paper No. 8. Table 1.20c, p. 47.

Figure 4

NET POPULATION GROWTH AND CONTRIBUTION FROM IMMIGRATION
AUSTRALIA, 1951 TO 1991
At June 30

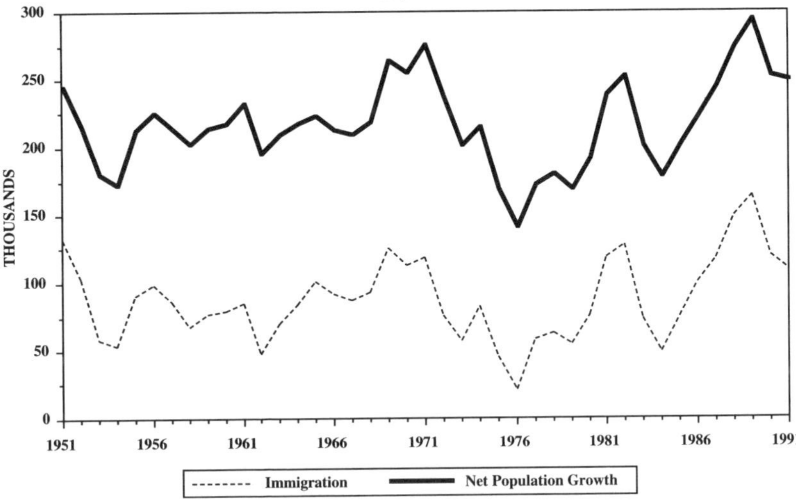

Sources: Australian Economic Statistics: 2949-50 to 1989-90, by RA Foster and S Stewart. Reserve Bank of Australia. Occasional Paper No. 8. Table 4.1, p. 149.
Australian Economic Indicators. ABS Cat . No. 1350.0. Table 8.9, p.93.

Figure 5

SAVING, INVESTMENT AND CURRENT ACCOUNT DEFICIT AS A % OF GDP

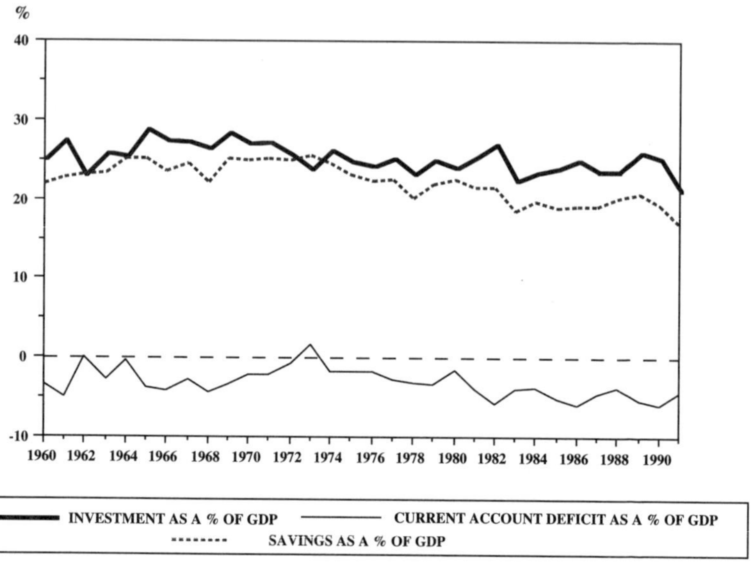

Source: Australian National Accounts National Income and Expenditure, March Q. 1991. ABS Cat. No. 5206.0.
Table 48, Gross Domestic Product at Current Prices.
Australian National Accounts: National Income and Expenditure, 1989-90. ABS Cat No. 5204.0.
Table 59, Gross Fixed Capital Expenditure, by Type of Asset. Table 61, Increase in Stocks. Table 71, Value of Main Aggregates at Current Pr
Balance of Payments, Australia, Dec. Q. 1991. ABS Cat. No. 5302.0. Table 2, Current Account - Summary.
Balance of Payments, Australia, 1990-91. ABS Cat. No. 5303.0. Table 2, Current Account - Summary. Table 27, Current Account - Summary.

Figure 6
AVERAGE UNEMPLOYMENT RATE, 1964-1991
AUSTRALIA AND OECD

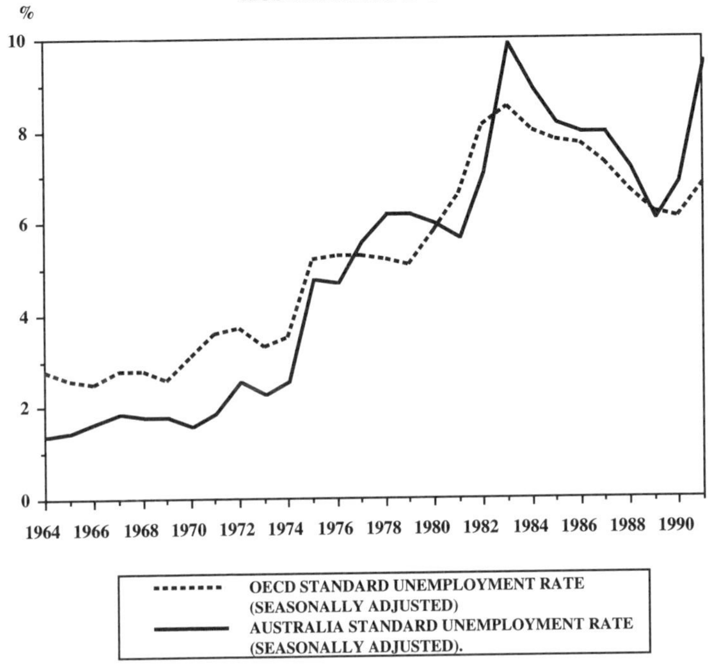

Source: OECD Main Economic Indicators Database. Reuters Numeric Services

Figure 7
NET PRIVATE WEALTH AS % GDP, AUSTRALIA
1969/70 TO 1990/91
Year end June 30

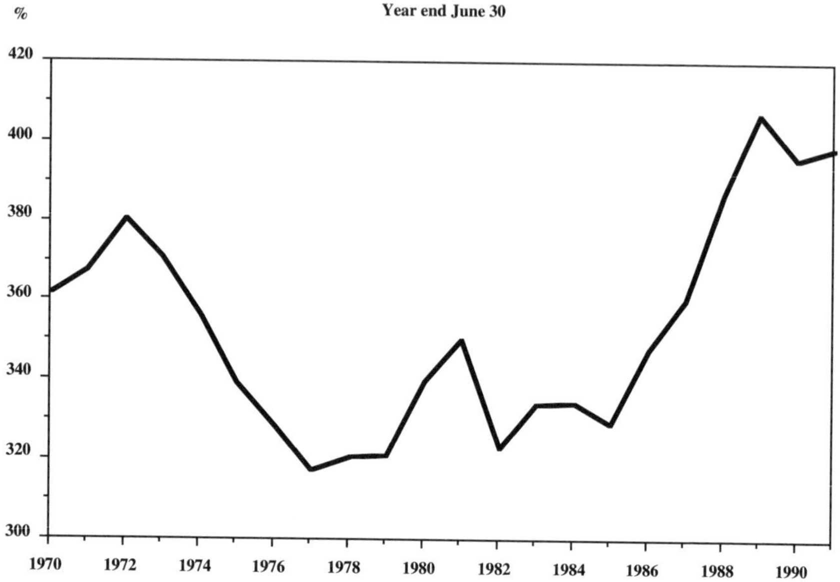

Source: Economic Round-up, Summer 1991. Dept. of The Treasury. Canberra, AGPS, 1991. p. 15.
Table 1: Private Sector Wealth at Market Prices

Table 1
GDP PER HEAD, AT AVERAGE OECD PRICES USING PURCHASING POWER PARITIES (US DOLLARS)

	1970	1980	1990
USA	4 919	11 794	21 449
SWITZERLAND	5 351	12 087	20 997
LUXEMBOURG	3 919	9 610	19 340
CANADA	3 733	10 509	19 120
GERMANY	3 884	10 170	18 291
JAPAN	2 932	8 225	17 634
FRANCE	3 696	9 740	17 431
SWEDEN	3 986	9 517	16 867
DENMARK	3 724	9 085	16 765
AUSTRIA	3 158	9 081	16 620
FINLAND	3 007	8 342	16 453
BELGIUM	3 310	9 076	16 405
ITALY	3 123	8 743	16 021
AUSTRALIA	3 644	9 003	15 951
NORWAY	2 812	8 622	15 921
ICELAND	2 764	9 448	15 851
NETHERLANDS	3 699	9 233	15 766
UK	3 399	8 259	15 720
NEW ZEALAND	3 474	7 836	13 258
SPAIN	2 366	6 126	11 792
PORTUGAL	1 545	4 511	8 389
IRELAND	1 853	5 190	10 659
GREECE	1 507	4 426	7 349
TURKEY	628	1 673	3 316

Source: Gross Domestic Product at Purchasing Power Parity in OECD Countries, 1990. ABS cat. no. 5226.0 Table 5. Gross Domestic Product per Head, at average OECD Prices using Purchasing Power Parities (US Dollars)

Table 2
REAL GDP/GNP PER EMPLOYEE
Constant 1980 US dollars, adjusted by purchasing-power parities

	1970	1980	1990
USA	26 148	27 050	29 394
NETHERLANDS	19 532	25400	28 495
CANADA	21 321	24 569	27 538
ITALY	16 223	22 149	26 289
FRANCE	16 336	21 414	25 615
BELGIUM	15 718	21 265	24 960
NORWAY	14 806	20 131	24 881
LUXEMBOURG	17 544	20 952	24 152
SWITZERLAND	18 398	20 806	23 143
GERMANY	15 575	20 254	23 143
SPAIN	12 308	18 276	22 254
JAPAN	11 486	16 587	21 655
AUSTRIA	13 157	18 178	21 213
AUSTRALIA	16 156	19 449	20 996
UK	14 842	17 632	20 659
FINLAND	11 933	16 280	20 615
ICELAND	15 015	21 719	20 461
SWEDEN	16 244	17 898	20 025
IRELAND	10 072	14 619	19 908
DENMARK	14 810	17 609	19 868
NEW ZEALAND	15 453	15 654	17 531
GREECE	8 785	12 992	13 543
PORTUGAL	7 609	10 159	11 426
TURKEY	5 662	8 043	10 586

Table 3
REAL NATIONAL DISPOSABLE INCOME PER CAPITA, AUSTRALIA 1960/61 – 1989/90

	GDP per capita	National Disposable Income (NDI) (a) per capita	NDI as a proportion of GDP	NDI per capita adjusted for Terms of Trade
	(Percentage change on year earlier)			
1960/61	0.7	0.3	86.3	–0.3
1961/62	–0.5	–1.1	85.7	–0.8
1962/63	4.5	4.7	85.9	4.9
1963/64	5.0	5.3	86.1	7.0
1964/65	5.0	5.2	86.3	4.2
1965/66	0.5	–0.2	85.7	–0.3
1966/67	4.4	4.4	85.6	4.2
1967/68	2.7	2.5	85.5	1.9
1968/69	5.7	6.1	85.8	6.3
1969/70	4.2	3.8	85.5	4.6
1970/71	2.8	2.8	85.5	0.9
1971/72	2.0	1.8	85.4	1.5
1972/73	2.8	2.5	85.0	5.7
1973/74	3.0	3.3	85.3	4.3
1974/75	–0.2	–0.6	84.9	–2.0
1975/76	1.3	0.4	84.2	–0.4
1976/77	1.8	1.7	84.1	1.3
1977/78	–0.3	–0.6	83.8	–2.2
1978/79	3.9	3.9	83.8	4.3
1979/80	1.2	1.2	83.8	1.8
1980/81	1.9	1.9	83.8	1.6
1981/82	–0.1	–1.1	82.9	–1.4
1982/83	–2.8	–4.0	81.9	–4.2
1983/84	4.3	4.4	82.0	4.8
1984/85	4.1	3.8	81.8	3.3
1985/86	2.5	2.8	82.0	1.0
1986/87	0.9	0.9	82.0	–0.1
1987/88	3.1	3.0	81.9	4.8
1988/89	2.2	1.1	81.0	3.9
1989/90	1.8	1.0	80.4	0.6
Annual average				
30 years to:				
1989/90	2.3	2.0	84.1	2.0
7 years to:				
1981/82	1.4	1.0	83.8	0.7
1989/90	2.7	2.4	81.6	2.6
10 years to:				
1969/70	3.2	3.1	85.8	3.1
1979/80	1.8	1.6	84.6	1.5
1989/90	1.8	1.3	82.0	1.4

Source: *Economic Round–up, Summer 1990. Australia. Dept. of The Treasury. Canberra, AGPS, 1990, p. 14. Table 1: Measures of Living Standards (1984–85 Prices)*

BIBLIOGRAPHY

Aaron, H.J. (1984), 'Social welfare in Australia', in Caves & Krause (eds), *The Australian Economy*, Allen & Unwin, Sydney.

Abelson, P. (1987), 'Fairness in the real world', *Australian Economic Papers*, 26 (48), June.

Ackland, R. (1987), 'Fairness in the real world', *Australian Economic Papers*, 26 (48), June.

Argy, F. (1990), 'Immigration and the current account deficit' in Easson, M. (ed.), *Australia and Immigration*, Pluto Press.

Argy, F. (1991), *Australia's competitive handicaps: how far are governments to blame?*

Argy, V. (1992), *Australian macroeconomic policy in a changing world environment 1973–1990*, Allen & Unwin.

Australian Bureau of Agricultural Economics (1992), *Greenhouse policies and the Australian aluminium industry*, ABARE.

Australian Bureau of Statistics (1992), *Productivity, prices, profits and pay 1964–65 to 1989–90*, ABS catalogue No. 5239.0.

Australian Commission for the Future (1991), *Energy Futures*, CFF Research Paper, 11/91.

Banks, G. et al. (1991), 'Export Performance' in Gruen, F.H., *Australian Economic Policy*, Centre for Economic Policy Research (CEPR), Australian National University (ANU).

Berry, M.J. (1987), 'Inequality' in S.Encel & M.Berry (eds), *Selected Readings in Australian Society*, Longman.

Borland, J. (1990), 'Unemployment in Australia', *Australian Economic Review*, 1st Q.

Bradbury, B. (1990) *Modelling the impact of labour market changes on the distribution of family incomes*, Social Policy Research Centre, University of NSW.

Bradbury, B. et al. (1990), *Trends in the Disposable Incomes of Australian Families*, SPRC Discussion Paper No.16, Social Policy Research Centre, University of NSW .

Bradbury, B. and Doyle, J. (1991), *Family Incomes and Economic Growth in the 1980s*, Social Policy Research Centre, University of NSW.

Browning, E.K. (1987), 'On the marginal welfare cost of taxation', *American Economic Review*, vol. 77.

Callen, T. (1991), *Estimates of Private Sector Wealth*, RBA Discussion Paper 9109.

Carruther, D.S. (1992), *The significance of the 1992 UN Conference on Environment*, Address to CEDA, 29 January 1992.

Castles, F.G. & Mumford, K. (1992), *The Vision of Full Employment Australia*, Public Policy Program, ANU.

Castles, F.G. (1989), 'Social protection by other means' in Castles (ed.), *Comparative History of Public Policy*, Polity Press.

Castles, I. (1992), 'Living standards in Sydney and Japanese cities—a comparison' in Sheridan (ed.), *The Australian economy in the Japanese mirror*, University of Queensland Press.

Centre for International Economics (1991), *Securing sustainable development*, CIE.

Chapman, B.J. et al. (1991), 'Perspectives on Australian Unemployment' in Gruen, F.H., *Australian Economic Policy*, CEPR, ANU.

Chapman, B.J. et al. (1991), *Analysing the impact of consensual incomes policy*, Discussion Paper No. 253, CEPR, ANU.

Chapman, B.J. et al. (1992), *Long term unemployment: projections and policy*, ANU.

Chouraqui, J.C. et al. (1986), *Public Debt in a medium term perspective*, OECD Economic Studies No. 7, Autumn.

Clarnette, W. et al. (1988), *Wealth and Poverty*, IPA Policy Issues No. 6.

Corden, W.M. (1988), *Australian Macroeconomic Experience*, Discussion Paper 194, CEPR, ANU.

Crafts, N. (1991), *Reversing relative economic decline?*, Oxford Review of Economic Policy, Vol. 7, No. 3.

CSIRO Institute of Natural Resources & Environment (undated), *Australia's environment and its natural resources*, CSIRO, Canberra.

Department of Employment, Education and Training (1991), *Australian Work Force in year 2001*, AGPS.

Dilnot, A. (1990), *From most to least*, Australian Society, 7/90.

Dilnot, A. (1990), 'The distribution and composition of personal sector wealth', *Australian Economic Review*, 1st Q.

Dowrick, S. (1990), *Why did the productivity of labour grow slower in the 80s*, Centre for Economic Policy Research, Discussion Paper No. 232.

Dwyer, J. (1990), *Australia's Traded Goods Sector*, Paper to 19th Conf. of Economists, University of NSW, Sept.

Ecologically Sustainable Development Working Party (1991), *Final report executive summaries*, November 1991, AGPS.

Economic Planning Advisory Council (EPAC):

CP 35: *Income support policies*, Oct. 1988.

CP 39: *Productivity in Aust.*, April 1989.

CP 40: *Trends in household debt*, Sept.1989.

DP 90/04: *Towards a more coop. federalism*, June 1990.

CP 43: *Australia's capital needs in the 1990s*.

CP 44: *Size and Efficiency of the Public Sector*, Nov. 1990.
CP 46: *Urban and regional issues*, Jan. 1991.
BP 10: *Background Papers on Urban & Regional Issues.*
CP 47: *Competitiveness: the policy environment*, April 1991.
CP 50: *Current account adjustment options for the 1990s*, May 1992.
BP 16: *Pricing and management of natural resources*, Nov. 1991.

Edey, M. & Britten-Jones, M. (1990), *Australian Macro-economic policy in the 80s*, RBA Conference Proceedings.

Freebairn, J. (1990), *Effective real tax rates*, EPAC Background Paper No. 3, Oct.

Gruen, F.H. (1986), *How bad is Australia's economic performance and why?* Economic Record, July.

Harris, S. (1991), *Ecologically sustainable development: implications for the policy process*, AIPA Conference, 9 December 1991.

Industry Commission (1991), *Annual Report* 1990–91, AGPS, Canberra.

Intergovernmental Panel on Climate Change (1990), *Climate change*, Cambridge University Press, Cambridge.

Isaac, J.E. (1988), *The distribution of productivity gains*, EPAC Discussion Paper 88 06.

Jonson, P.D. (1991), 'Australia's economy' in Appleyard (ed.), *Western Australia*, St George Books.

Kakwani, N. (1991), 'Aggregate welfare and growth rates' in Johnson, M.R. et al. (eds), *Contemporary issues in Australian economics*, Macmillan.

Kasper, W. et al. (1980), *Australia at the crossroads*, Harcourt Brace Jovanovich, Australia.

Keating, M. & Dixon, G. (1989), *Making economic policy in Australia*, Longman Cheshire, Melbourne.

Keating, M.S. (1992), *Australia's economic prospects*, address to Economic Society Forecasting Conference, Melbourne.

Keynes, J.M., (1919), *The economic consequences of the peace*, Macmillan, London.

Lane, J. & Ersson, S. (1990), *Comparative Political Economy*, Pinter.

Lindbeck, A. (1986), *Limits to the welfare state*, Challenge, Jan/Feb.

Little, I.M.D. (1960), *A critique of welfare economics*, Oxford University Press.

London Economics (1992), *The impact of global warming control policies on Australian industry*, London Economics 1/92.

Maddock, R. & McLean, I. (eds) (1987), *The Australian economy in the long run*, Cambridge University Press, New York.

Makin, T., *Exportables, importables and the terms of trade*, Economic Papers.

Marsh, I. (1991), *Implementation: building Australian orientations and attitudes in internationalising Australia's economy*, Australian Graduate School of Management, July 1990.

McKibbon, W.J. & Morling, S. (1991), 'Macroeconomic policy' in Gruen, F.H. (ed.) *Australian Economic Policy*, CEPR, ANU.

Milbourne, R. (1991), *Growth, capital accumulation and foreign debt*, University of NSW, 9/91.

Minford, P. (1988), 'Arbitration, collective bargaining and the wage structure', *Growth* 33, Sept.

Moore, D. (1990), 'Australia pays the price of consensus', *Asian Wall Street Journal*, August.

Mulvey, C. (1986), 'Arbitration, collective bargaining and the wage structure', *Growth* 33, September.

Nomura Research Institute (1989), *Medium-term economic outlook for Japan and the world*, Tokyo.

Nordhaus, W.D. (1991), 'To slow or not to slow: the economics of the greenhouse effect', *Economic Journal* 7/91 .

Norris, K. (1986), 'The wages structure: does arbitration make any difference?' in Niland, J. (ed.), *Wage fixation in Australia*, Allen & Unwin, Sydney.

Nevile, J.W. (1991), 'Immigration and macroeconomic performance in Australia', *Growth* 39, CEDA, Melbourne.

Parmenter, B.R. et al. (1991), 'A reinterpretation of the CIE Projections of the long run economic effects of immigration', *Economic Record*, December.

Phipps, T. et al. (1992), *The slowdown in Australian productivity growth*, Department of Economics, University of Sydney.

Pitchford, J. (1992), *Macroeconomic policy: issues for the 1990s*, National Farmers Federation Discussion Paper.

Rawls, J. (1971), *A theory of justice*, Harvard .

Shann, E.W. (1984), *The size of the mineral sector*, Working papers 12 and 13, Centre for Resource & Environmental Studies, ANU.

Saunders, P. (1990), 'Income inequality in Australia', in Income Distribution Seminar, Papers and Proceedings, Economic and Social Policy Group.

Saunders, P. et al. (1989), 'Income inequality in Australia and New Zealand', SWRC Discussion Paper No. 15, SWRC, University of NSW.

Schott, K. (1984), *Policy, Power and Order*, Yale University Press.

Smeeding, T. (1988–89), 'Poverty, affluence, and the income costs of children', *Journal of Post-Keynesian economics*, 11 (2), Winter.

Stemp, P.J. (ed.) (1991), *Saving and Policy*, Centre for Economic Policy Research, ANU.

Stilwell, F. (1992), *Economic Inequality*, paper prepared for CEDA.

Treasury, Commonwealth (1990), 'Movements in living standards and the role of microeconomic policy', *Round Up*, Summer.

Treasury, Commonwealth (1990), 'Trends in aggregate wealth', *Round Up*, Summer.

Treasury, Commonwealth (1992), 'Trends in Productivity', *Round Up*, Autumn.

Walsh, P. (1991), 'Errors and achievements, economic policy in the 1980s', *The 1991 Shann Memorial Lecture*, University of WA, Discussion Paper.

White, G. (1991), *Monetary Policy in the 1980s*, IPA Conference, December.

White, G. (1991), *Determinants of Saving in the Australian economy*, 20th Conference of Economists.

White, G. (1992), *A vision for Australia: how should such a vision be expressed?*, Paper prepared for CEDA.

CEDA Advisory Committee

Supriya Singh, Research Fellow, Centre for International Research on Communication and Information Technologies
Dr Robin Stewardson, Chief Economist, The Broken Hill Proprietary Co Ltd
Louise Wilson, Finance and Banking Analyst

Queensland

Don Boyd, Managing Partner, Sly & Weigall Cannan & Peterson
John Maguire, Managing Director, Driza-Bone Pty Ltd
Brian McCafferty, Senior Partner, Morris Fletcher & Cross
Alan Midwood, Managing Director, Rider Hunt Gold Coast Pty Ltd

South Australia

John Goodman, Chairman and Chief Executive, Baulderstone Hornibrook

Western Australia

Professor Reg Appleyard, Professor of Economic History, University of Western Australia
Steven Cole, Managing Partner, Parker & Parker
Dr John Wood, Executive Director, Strategic Development Division, State Development Western Australia.

Tasmania

Bob Graham, Honorary Director, CEDA
Paul Kemp, Managing Director, The Trust Bank

Economist Advisory Committee

Melbourne

Chairman

Dr Robin Stewardson, Chief Economist, The Broken Hill Proprietary Company Limited

Dr Peter Brain, Executive Director, National Institute of Economic and Industry Research
Dr Vince Fitzgerald, Executive Director, The Allen Consulting Group
Professor John Freebairn, Monash University
Ian Little, Chief Economist, ANZ Banking Group Limited
Charles Maceck, Managing Director—Investment Management, Country Natwest Australia Ltd
John Macleod, Chief Economist, CRA Limited
Dr Ed Shann, Access Economics

Sydney

Chairman

Paul McCarthy, Commonwealth Bank of Australia

Adrian Blundell-Wignall, Reserve Bank of Australia
Bill Evans, Chief Economist, Westpac Banking Corporation
Frank Gelber, BIS Shrapnel
Professor John Nevile, University of New South Wales
Bill Shields, Macquarie Bank
Dr Don Stammer, Bain & Company
Garry White, Corporate Investments

CEDA Office Bearers and Staff as at July 1992

President
Chairman, Research Advisory Council
R A Johnston, AC

Chairman, Board of Trustees and Vice President
E A Mayer
President, Business/Higher Education Roundtable

Chairman, Board of Directors
Dr W W J Uhlenbruch, AM
Chairman and Managing Director, Hella-Australia Pty Ltd

Immediate Past President
J W Utz, AC
Chairman, Rothmans Holdings Ltd

Emeritus Past President
D H Merry, OBE
Riddells Creek, Victoria

Emeritus Chairman, Board of Trustees
A C Goode
Chairman, The All-States Group

Executive Committee Joint Chairmen
I A Deveson
Chairman, HSV 7
J T Dominguez, AM
Chairman, SBC Dominguez Barry Ltd

Public Policy Education Committee Joint Chairmen
J B Burrows
Managing Partner Australia, Arthur Andersen & Co
L A Wilson
Chairman, Richardson Pacific Ltd

Conference Centre Management Committee Chairman
J Herbig
Managing Director, BFGoodrich Chemical Ltd

Research Management Committee Joint Chairmen
J H Curtis, CB
Chairman NorTel Australia Pty Ltd
J R Smith, AM
Chairman, State Electricity Commission of Victoria

Research Operations Committee Joint Chairmen
G S Davis, NSW
J Salter, Victoria

Membership Committee Joint Chairmen
D S Carruthers
Group Executive, CRA Ltd
I K Payne
Deputy Managing Director, Commonwealth Bank of Australia

Honorary Treasurer
L G C Moyle
Seville, Victoria

Honorary Comptroller
T D Cregan
Springvale, Victoria

Strategic Issues Forum Chairman
Sir John Mason, KCMG
Chairman, THORN EMI Australia Ltd

Strategic Issues Forum Deputy Chairman
J R Smith, AM
Chairman, State Electricity Commission of Victoria

Business Intelligence Unit Patrons
D S Greatorex, AO
Chairman, State Bank of NSW
L G C Moyle
Seville, Victoria

Business Intelligence Unit Chairman
L A Wilson
Chairman, Richardson Pacific Ltd

State Vice Presidents

New South Wales
R F E Warburton
Chief Executive, Du Pont (Australia) Ltd

Victoria
R Fynmore
Executive General Manager Corporate Development, The Broken Hill Proprietary Co Ltd

Queensland
R Deicke, CMG
Chairman, Bundaberg Sugar Company Ltd

South Australia
M A Kinnaird, AO
Chairman, Kinhill Engineers Pty Ltd

Western Australia
K A Pownall
Chairman, Esri Pty Ltd

Tasmania
P Kemp
Managing Director, The Trust Bank

Operating Committee

Chairman and Chief Counsellor
Dr Peter Grey, AM

Deputy Chairman and Executive Director
Noel Claire Morgan

Vice-Chairmen (Victoria)
Peter Barnett, AM
E H (Mal) Draeger

Vice-Chairman (New South Wales)
Warren Reed

Company Secretary and Chief Accountant
Matt Kumar

Research Director
Dr John Leaper

Executive Director—Queensland
Jan McMaster

Regional Director—Southern
Toni Steinbrecher

Honorary Director—South Australia
Silvija Footner

Honorary Secretary—Western Australia
Michele Connolly

Honorary Director—Tasmania
R J Graham

Associate Director—Sydney
Cynthia Coppock

Associate Director—Melbourne
Jeanette Periera

CEDA International Affiliates

Close relationships have been developed with independent, non-political research organisations in other countries. These organisations are composed of businessmen and scholars, have objectives similar to those of CEDA, and pursue them by similarly objective methods. In several cases, agreements for reciprocal distribution of publications have developed out of this cooperation.

CE	Circulo de Empresarios, Serrano Jover 5–2, Madrid 28015, Spain
CED	Committee for Economic Development, 1700 K Street NW, Washington DC 20006, USA
CEPES	Vereinigung fur wirtschaftlichen Fortschritt e.V, Weissfrauenstrasse 9, 6000 Frankfurt 11, Germany
FAE	Forum de Administradores de Empresas, Av. Julio Dinis, 10–2–G, 1000, Lisbon, Portugal
IDEP	Institut de L'Entreprise, 6 rue Clement Marot, 75008, Paris, France
IDW	Institut der Deutschen Wirtschaft, Gustav-Heinemann-Ufer 84–88, 5000 Cologne 51, Germany
IE	Institute of the Enterprise, Rue de la Concorde 53, 1060, Brussels, Belgium
IEA	Institute of Economic Affairs, 2 Lord North Street, London, SW1P 3LB, England
KEIZAI DOYUKAI	Japan Association of Corporate Executives, Yusen Building, 3–2 Marunouchi, 2-chome, Chiyoda-Ku, Tokyo, Japan
SNS	Center for Business and Policy Studies, Skoldungagatan 2, Stockholm, Sweden

CEDA Direct Correspondent Network

P. T. Redeco
Gendung Patra, 1st Floor, JL Jend. Gato Subroto 32.34, Jakarta, Indonesia

European Policy Forum
Premier House, 10 Greycoat Place, London, SW1P 1SB, England

Institute of South-east Asian Studies
Heng Mui Kkeng Terrace, Singapore 0511

ISIS Malaysia (Institute of Strategic and International Studies)
No.1 Pesiaran Sultan Salahuddin, P O Box 12424, Kuala Lumpur, Malaysia

Institute of Policy Studies
Victoria University of Wellington, P O Box 600, Wellington, New Zealand

Institute for Research on Public Policy
3771 Haro Road, Victoria, British Columbia V8W 2Y2, Canada

Philippine Institute for Development Studies
4th Floor, Neda Sa Makata Building, Legaspi Village, Makat, Metro Manila, The Philippines

Enquiries for publications should be addressed to the Librarian,
Committee for Economic Development of Australia,
CEDA House, 123 Lonsdale Street, Melbourne.
Telephone: (03) 662 3544 Facsimile: (03) 663 7271.